FOR SERVICES RENDERED

A Play in Three Acts

by W. Somerset Maugham

samuelfrench.co.uk

FOR AMATEUR PRODUCTION ENQUIRIES

UNITED KINGDOM AND WORLD
EXCLUDING NORTH AMERICA
plays@samuelfrench.co.uk
020 7255 4302/01

Each title is subject to availability from Samuel French,
depending upon country of performance.

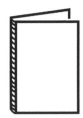

Other plays by W. SOMERSET MAUGHAM
published and licensed by Samuel French

Home and Beauty

The Circle

The Constant Wife

The Noble Spaniard

FIND PERFECT PLAYS TO PERFORM AT
www.samuelfrench.co.uk/perform

ABOUT THE AUTHOR

W Somerset Maugham was born in Paris in 1874. He trained as a doctor in London where he started writing his first novels. He achieved fame in 1907 with the production of *Lady Friedrich*, and by 1908 he had four plays running simultaneously in London.

In 1947 Maugham instituted the Somerset Maugham Award for best British writer(s) under the age of thirty-five for a fictional work published within the last year. Notable winners have included Thom Gunn, V.S. Naipaul and both Kingsley and Martin Amis.

Upon his death in 1965, Maugham donated his royalties to the Royal Literary Fund.

Maugham remains a hugely influential writer whose works have been adapted for film, television, radio and theatre.

Notable works include:-
Novels:
The Magician (1908/09); *Of Human Bondage* (1915);
The Moon and Sixpence (1919); *The Painted Veil* (1925);
Christmas Holiday (1939); *The Razor's Edge* (1943/44);
Short Stories: *Rain* (1921); *Footprints in the Jungle* (1927);
Plays: *East of Suez* (1922); *Home and Beauty* (1923);
The Constant Wife (1926); *The Lotus Eater* (1935)

FOR SERVICES RENDERED

First produced at the Globe Theatre, London, W.I., on 1 November 1932, with the following cast of characters:

LEONARD ARDSLEY	C.V. France
CHARLOTTE ARDSLEY (his wife)	Louise Hampton
SYDNEY (his son)	Cedric Hardwicke
EVA } (his unmarried daughters)	{ Flora Robson
LOIS	Marjoria Mars
ETHEL BARTLETT (his married daughter)	Diana Hamilton
HOWARD BARTLETT (her husband)	W. Cronin-Wilson
COLLIE STRATTON (Commander, R.N.)	Ralph Richardson
WILFRED CEDAR	S. J. Warmington
GWEN CEDAR (his wife)	Marda Vanne
DR. PRENTICE (Mrs Ardsley's brother)	David Hawthorne
GERTRUDE (the Ardsleys' parlour maid)	Phyllis Shand

The Play was produced by H.K. Ayliff

SYNOPSIS OF SCENES

The action of the play takes place in the Ardsleys' house at Rambleston, a small country town in Kent, near the cathedral city of Stanbury.

ACT I
The Garden Terrace.   An afternoon in September.

ACT II
The Dining Room.   After lunch. About two weeks later.

ACT III
The Drawing Room.   The next day.

ACT I

SCENE—A terrace at the back of the **ARDSLEYS'** *house.
It is five o'clock on a warm afternoon in September.*

*French windows lead out on it from the house, and
beyond is the garden. See the Ground Plan.*

LEONARD ARDSLEY *is the only solicitor in Rambleston
and his house faces the village street. Part of it is used
as his office. Tea is laid.*

MRS ARDSLEY *is sitting on the seat, 2, hemming a
napkin. She is a thin, grey-haired woman of more than
sixty, with a severe face but kind eyes. She is quietly
dressed.* **GERTRUDE,** *the maid, brings in the tea.*

MRS ARDSLEY Is it tea-time?

GERTRUDE *(bringing the tea-tray to the table)* The church clock's
striking now, ma'am.

MRS ARDSLEY Go down to the tennis court and tell them that
tea is ready.

GERTRUDE Very good, ma'am. *(She crosses down right)*

MRS ARDSLEY *(putting her sewing aside)* Have you told
Mr. Sydney? *(She rises)*

GERTRUDE *(turning at right)* Yes, ma'am.

She exits right.

MRS ARDSLEY *crosses up and brings chairs 4 and 5
to the table.* **SYDNEY** *comes in from the house. He is a
heavy man of hard on forty, with a big, fat face. He is*

*blind and walks with a stick, but he knows his way
about and moves with little hesitation.*

MRS ARDSLEY *(by chair 6)* Where would you like to sit, dear?

SYDNEY Anywhere.

*He lets himself down into chair 4, right of the table and
puts down his stick.*

MRS ARDSLEY *(sitting in chair 6)* What have you been doing
all the afternoon?

SYDNEY Nothing very much. Knitting a bit.

MRS ARDSLEY Ethel's here. Howard's coming to fetch her on his
way home from Stanbury. He's gone to the cattle-market.

SYDNEY *(after a slight pause)* I suppose he'll be as tight as a
drum.

MRS ARDSLEY Sydney!

SYDNEY *(with a little chuckle)* What rot it all is. Does Ethel
really think we don't know he drinks?

MRS ARDSLEY She's proud. She doesn't want to admit that she
made a mistake.

SYDNEY I shall never stop asking myself what on earth she
saw in him.

MRS ARDSLEY Everything was so different then. He looked
very nice in uniform. He was an officer.

SYDNEY You and father ought to have put your foot down.

MRS ARDSLEY They were madly in love with one another.
When all that slaughter was going on it seemed so
snobbish to object to a man because he was just a small
tenant farmer.

SYDNEY Did you think the war was going on for ever?

MRS ARDSLEY No, but it looked as though the world would be
a changed place when it stopped.

SYDNEY *(after a moment)* It's funny when you think of it. Everything goes on in the same old way, except that we're all broke to the wide and a few hundred thousand fellows like me have had our chance of making a good job of life snatched away from us.

MRS ARDSLEY *gives a sigh and makes an unhappy gesture.* SYDNEY *utters a little sardonic chuckle.*

Cheer up, mother. You must console yourself by thinking that you've got a hero for a son. M.C. and mentioned in dispatches. No one can say I didn't do my bit.

MRS ARDSLEY They're just coming.

GWEN CEDAR *and* ETHEL BARTLETT *enter right from the garden.* ETHEL BARTLETT, MRS ARDSLEY's *second daughter, is a handsome woman of thirty-five, with regular features and fine eyes.* GWEN CEDAR *is fifty, a good deal painted, with dyed hair; she is too smartly dressed in a manner hardly becoming to her age. She has the mechanical brightness of a woman who is desperately hanging on to the remains of her youth.*

ETHEL *(crossing left)* The others are coming as soon as they've finished the set. Hulloa, Sydney. *(She moves down below chair 7)*

SYDNEY Hulloa.

GWEN *(having moved across to right of* SYDNEY; *shaking hands with him)* How are you to-day, Sydney? You're looking very well.

SYDNEY Oh, I'm all right, thanks.

GWEN Busy as a bee as usual, I suppose. You're simply amazing.

MRS ARDSLEY *(trying to head her off)* Let me give you some tea.

GWEN *(moving to left of chair 5)* I do admire you. I mean, you must have great strength of character.

SYDNEY *(with a grin)* A will of iron.

GWEN *(sitting in chair 5)* I remember when I was ill last spring and they kept me in a darkened room for nearly a week, it was quite intolerable. But I kept on saying to myself, well, it's nothing compared to what poor Sydney has to put up with.

SYDNEY And you were right.

MRS ARDSLEY One lump of sugar?

GWEN Oh, no, I never take sugar. It's Lent all the year round for me. *(Brightly attacking* SYDNEY *again)* It's a marvel to me how you pass the time.

SYDNEY Charming women like you are very sweet to me, and my sisters are good enough to play chess with me. I improve my mind by reading.

ETHEL *sits in chair 8.*

GWEN Oh, yes, Braille. I love reading. I always read at least one novel a day. Of course I've got a head like a sieve. D'you know, it's oftened happened to me to read a novel right through and never remember till the end that I'd read it before. It always makes me so angry. I mean, it's such a waste of time.

A slight pause.

SYDNEY How's the farm, Ethel?

ETHEL We're making the most of the fine weather.

GWEN It must be so interesting, living on a farm. Making butter and all that sort of thing.

ETHEL One's at it from morning till night. It keeps one from thinking.

GWEN But of course you have people to do all the rough work for you.

ETHEL What makes you think that?

GWEN You don't mean to say you do it yourself. How on earth d'you keep your hands?

ETHEL *(with a glance at them, smiling)* I don't.

There is a sound of voices from the garden.

MRS ARDSLEY *(looking across right)* Here are the others.

*Her two other daughters, **EVA** and **LOIS**, enter right, with the two men they have been playing tennis with. These are **WILFRED CEDAR** and **COLLIE STRATTON**. **WILFRED CEDAR** is a stout, elderly man but well preserved, with a red face and grey, crisply-curling hair. He is stout, jovial, breezy and sensual. He is out to enjoy all the good things of life. **COLLIE STRATTON** is between thirty-five and forty. He has been in the Royal Navy and has the rather school-boyish manner of those men who have never quite grown-up. He has a pleasant frank look. **EVA** is **MRS ARDSLEY**'s eldest daughter. She is thin and of a somewhat haggard appearance. She is very gentle, a trifle subdued, but she does not give you the impression of being at peace with herself. Behind the placidity is a strange restlessness. She is thirty-nine. **LOIS ARDSLEY** is the youngest of the family. She is twenty-six, but the peaceful, monotonous life she has led has preserved her youth and she looks little more than twenty. She is gay and natural. She is a very pretty young woman, but what is even more attractive in her than her blue eyes and straight nose is the air she has of immense healthiness.*

LOIS *(as she crosses)* Tea. Tea. Tea. *(She moves above the table to chair 7)*

WILFRED *(moving to right of **SYDNEY**)* By George, they made us run about. Hulloa, Sydney.

COLLIE moves down below the seat, 2. EVA remains near the entrance right.

MRS ARDSLEY How were you playing?

WILFRED Lois and me against Eva and Collie.

EVA Of course Wilfred's in a different class from us.

COLLIE That forehand drive of yours is devilish.

WILFRED I've had a lot of practice, you know, playing in tournaments on the Riviera and so on.

GWEN Of course he was too old for singles, but a few years ago he was one of the best doubles players in Cannes.

WILFRED *(not too pleased)* I don't know that I play any worse than I played a few years ago.

GWEN Well, you can't expect to get across the court as you used to when you were young. I mean, that's silly.

WILFRED Gwen always talks as if I was a hundred. What I say is, a woman's as old as she looks and a man as old as he feels.

SYDNEY It has been said before.

MRS ARDSLEY *(to* WILFRED*)* How do you like your tea?

LOIS Oh, mother, I'm sure they want a drink.

WILFRED Clever girl.

MRS ARDSLEY What would you like?

WILFRED *(moving a little right)* Well, a glass of beer sounds good to me. What about you, Collie? *(He turns chair 3 to face a little left)*

COLLIE Suits me.

EVA *(moving up center)* I'll tell Gertrude.

MRS ARDSLEY *(as* EVA *is going)* Tell your father that if he wants any tea he'd better come now.

EVA Very well.

She goes off center, into the house.

WILFRED *(sitting in chair 3)* Damned convenient for your husband having his office in the house.

LOIS He's got a private door so that he can slip away without the clients seeing him.

GWEN Evie's looking a little tired, I think.

MRS ARDSLEY She's been rather nervy lately. I've wanted her uncle to have a look at her, but she won't let him.

GWEN So sad the man she was engaged to being killed in the war.

MRS ARDSLEY They were very much in love with one another.

ETHEL She's never really got over it, poor dear.

GWEN Pity she never found anyone else she liked.

MRS ARDSLEY In a place like this she could hardly hope to. By the end of the war there were very few young men left. And girls were growing up all the time.

GWEN I heard there *was* someone.

MRS ARDSLEY Not very desirable. I believe he did ask her, but she refused him.

GWEN I'm told he wasn't quite, quite. It's always a mistake to marry out of one's own class. It's never a success.

GWEN *has dropped a brick.* ETHEL *has married beneath her.*

LOIS Oh, what nonsense. As if that sort of thing mattered any more. It depends on the people, not on their class.

GWEN *suddenly realises what she has said, gives* ETHEL *a hurried look and tries to make everything right.*

GWEN Oh, of course. I didn't mean that. All sorts of people keep shops nowadays and go in for poultry farming and things like that. I don't mind what a man is as long as he's a gentleman.

COLLIE It's a relief to hear you say that, as I run a garage.

GWEN *(rising and easing right)* That's just what I mean. It doesn't matter your running a garage. *(Moving up to left of the french windows)* After all you were in the Navy and you commanded a destroyer.

SYDNEY To say nothing of having the D.S.O. and the Legion of Honour.

WILFRED In point of fact what made you go into the motor business, Collie?

COLLIE I had to do something. I was a pretty good mechanic. I got a bonus, you know, and I thought I might just as well put it into that as anything else.

WILFRED I suppose you do pretty well out of the motor-buses.

COLLIE *(sitting in chair 2)* Lot of expenses, you know.

> **GERTRUDE** *enters from the house with two tankards of beer on a tray, and comes down between 2 and 3.*

WILFRED Look what's here.

> *He takes one of the tankards and takes a great pull at it.* **GERTRUDE** *gives the other tankard to* **COLLIE,** *who sits on seat 2.* **EVA** *re-enters up center.*

> **GERTRUDE** *exits.*

EVA Father's just coming. He wants to see you, Collie.

COLLIE Oh, does he?

> **EVA** *moves to up left of the table.*

WILFRED That doesn't look too good, old man. When a solicitor wants to see you it's generally that he has something disagreeable to say to you.

LOIS Hurry up and finish your beer and we'll give them their revenge. It'll be getting dark soon.

> **WILFRED** *rises, and eases to right of chair 3.*

GWEN *(moving to above and left of* **WILFRED***)* Oh, are you going to play again, Wilfred? Don't you think it's time we went home?

WILFRED What's the hurry? You take the car. I'll have another set and I'll walk back.

GWEN Oh, if you're not coming, I'll wait.

WILFRED *(trying to hide his irritation behind his joviality)* Oh, come on, you can trust me out of your sight just this once. I promise to be a good boy.

A little look passes between them. She stifles a sigh and smiles brightly.

GWEN Oh, all right. A brisk walk won't do your figure any harm.

She turns towards **MRS ARDSLEY** *to say good-bye.*

MRS ARDSLEY *(rising)* I'll come as far as the door with you.

She joins **GWEN** *and they exit up center.*

SYDNEY Where's my stick, Evie?

EVA *moves round and gives it to him.*

(rising) I think I'll totter down to the court and see how you all play. *(He moves right)*

ETHEL *(rising and moving towards* **SYDNEY***)* I'll come with you, shall I?

EVA *(moving up center)* I think I'd better get some fresh tea for father.

LOIS *(up left)* Hurry up, then, or the light'll be going.

EVA I shan't be a minute.

She exits up center.

LOIS *(up left center)* What should we do in this house without Evie?

SYDNEY *(moving to the entrance right)* What would Evie do without us? You can't sacrifice yourself unless there's someone about whom you can sacrifice yourself for.

ETHEL *is at right center, on the left of* SYDNEY.

WILFRED You're a cynical bloke.

LOIS *(with a smile)* And ungrateful.

SYDNEY *(turning at right)* Not at all. It's jam for Evie to have an invalid to look after. If she could make me see by saying a magic word, d'you think she'd say it? Not on your life. Nature destined her to be a saint and it's damned lucky for her that I'm around to give her the opportunity of earning a heavenly crown.

ETHEL *(with a chuckle)* Come on, give me your arm.

SYDNEY *(putting on a cockney accent)* Spare a copper for a poor blind man, sir.

They go out right, to the garden.

LOIS *(starting to go right)* I'll just go and hunt for that ball. I think I know more or less where it is.

WILFRED I'd come with you if I weren't so lazy.

LOIS *(checking, between chairs 2 and 3)* No, stay there. You'll only wreck the flower beds with your big feet.

WILFRED I like that. I flatter myself not many men of my size have smaller feet than I have.

LOIS Modest fellow, aren't you? *(Moving right)* Give me a shout when Evie comes.

She exits right, into the garden.

WILFRED *(finishing his beer)* Good-looking girl that. Nice too. And she's got a head on her shoulders. *(He puts the tankard on the seat 2)*

COLLIE Plays a good game of tennis.

WILFRED Funny she shouldn't have been snapped up before now. If I was a young fellow and single I shouldn't hesitate.

COLLIE *(rising, and taking his tankard to the table, left)* She hasn't got much chance here, poor thing. Who the devil is there she can marry in a place like this?

WILFRED I wonder you don't have a cut in yourself.

COLLIE *(turning, below the table)* I'm fifteen years older than she is. And I haven't got a bean.

WILFRED Girls nowadays who live in the country have to take what they can get.

COLLIE Nothing doing as far as I'm concerned.

WILFRED *(with a shrewd look at him)* Oh!

COLLIE *(moving to left center)* Why d'you want to know?

WILFRED Only that she's a nice girl and I'd like to see her settled.

A pause.

COLLIE I say, old man, I suppose you wouldn't do me a favour.

WILFRED Of course I will, old boy. What is it?

COLLIE Well, to tell you the truth, I'm in a bit of a hole.

WILFRED Sorry to hear that. What's it all about?

COLLIE Business has been rotten lately.

WILFRED I know it has. And I don't know when things are going to improve. I can tell you I'm damned glad I got out when the going was good.

COLLIE I expect you are.

WILFRED Everyone told me I was a fool to retire. But I smelt a rat. I said, no, I've worked a good many years and I've made a packet. Now I'm going to live like a gentleman. I sold out at the top of the market. Just in time.

COLLIE *(moving away a pace or two)* Lucky.

WILFRED Lucky be damned. Clever, I call it.

COLLIE *(after a slight pause, turning back to* WILFRED*)* Look here, old man. I hate asking you, but I'm terribly hard up just now. I should be awfully grateful if you could lend me a bit.

WILFRED *(very heartily)* Why, my dear old boy, of course I will. I'm always glad to oblige a friend. How much d'you want?

COLLIE That's awfully kind of you. Could you manage two hundred pounds?

WILFRED *(after a slight hesitation)* Oh, I say, that's real money. I thought you were going to say a tenner. Two hundred pounds is quite another story.

COLLIE It's not very much for you.

WILFRED I'm not made of money, you know. My investments have gone down like everybody else's. Believe me, I haven't got more than I can spend.

COLLIE I'm in a most awful jam.

WILFRED Why don't you go to the bank?

COLLIE I'm overdrawn already. They won't lend me a bob.

WILFRED But haven't you got any security?

COLLIE Not that they'll accept.

WILFRED Then what d'you expect me to lend you the money on?

COLLIE I'll give you my word of honour to return it as soon as ever I can.

WILFRED *(rising and moving down right)* My dear old boy, you're a damned good chap and a D.S.O. and all that sort of thing, but this is business.

COLLIE You've known me for six months now. You must know I'm honest.

WILFRED *(turning, below the seat 2)* I took a furnished house down here for my wife's health, and when I heard you'd been in the navy of course I came to you for my petrol and tyres and repairs. I know it's hard for you fellows. I've paid all my bills on the nail.

COLLIE I've given you good service.

WILFRED I know you have. I'm very sorry your garage hasn't proved a good proposition. If you'd been a business man you'd have known it was crazy to settle down in a little tin-pot place like this. But I really don't see that I'm called upon to make you a present of two hundred pounds.

COLLIE I'm not asking it as a present.

WILFRED (*moving up between 2 and 3*) It comes to the same thing. I've lent dozens of fellows money and they never pay it back. I think it's a bit thick to ask me to lend you a sum like that.

COLLIE You don't think I like it. I tell you I'm absolutely up against it. It means life and death to me.

WILFRED I'm awfully sorry, old boy, but there's nothing doing. (*Glancing right*) ...I wonder if Lois has found that ball yet.

He turns right, and goes off into the garden.

COLLIE *sits in chair 4, dejectedly. In a moment* EVA *enters up center with the teapot.*

EVA What's the matter? You're looking terribly depressed.

COLLIE (*trying to collect himself*) I'm sorry. (*He rises and moves down right center*)

EVA *looks at him for a moment, then goes to above the table.*

EVA Are they waiting for us?

COLLIE (*with a slight sigh*) I suppose so.

A slight pause. Then EVA *moves towards* COLLIE, *to center.*

EVA Tell me what the matter is.

COLLIE *(turning and forcing a smile)* It wouldn't interest you.

EVA Why do you say that? Don't you know that anything that concerns you interests me.

COLLIE That's very sweet of you.

EVA I suppose I'm rather reserved. It's difficult for me to show my feelings. I should like you to look upon me as a friend.

COLLIE I do.

EVA *(sitting in chair 3)* Tell me what it is then. Perhaps I can help you.

COLLIE I'm afraid not. *(He sits on the seat 2)* I think you've got troubles enough of your own without sharing mine.

EVA You mean looking after Sydney. I don't look upon that as a trouble. I'm glad to do what I can for the poor boy. When I think of what the war did to him, it's only right that I should sacrifice myself.

COLLIE It's very good of you, all the same.

EVA You see, Ethel was married and Lois was so young. Mother isn't very strong. Looking after Sydney helped me to bear the loss of poor Ted.

COLLIE That was the man you were engaged to?

EVA Yes. I was terribly unhappy when he was killed. I'm afraid I was rather morbid about it. One can't afford to give in, can one? I mean, life is given to us, and it's our duty to make the best we can out of it.

COLLIE *(rather vaguely)* Naturally one gets over everything in course of time.

EVA Yes. I suppose one ought to consider oneself fortunate that one can. And I think a girl ought to marry, don't you?

I mean, it's a woman's province to have a home of her own and children to look after.

COLLIE Yes, I suppose it is. *(He rises, and moves to below and left of chair 4)*

There is a moment's pause.

EVA *(rising)* It's rather strange that you should never have married, Collie.

COLLIE *(turning to her with a grin)* I never had anything to marry on.

EVA Oh, money isn't everything. A clever woman can manage on very little. *(Brightly)* I must have a look round and see if I can't find someone to suit you.

COLLIE I'm afraid I'm too old now.

EVA Oh, what nonsense. You're just the same age as I am. Every woman loves a sailor. Between you and me and the gatepost I don't believe there's a girl here who wouldn't jump at the chance if you asked her.

COLLIE *(a trifle embarrassed)* I'm not likely to do that.

EVA *(after a slight pause)* Are you waiting for her to ask you? That's wanting almost too much.

COLLIE I suppose it is really.

EVA *(to above and right of chair 4)* After all, a nice girl can't do much more than show a man she's not indifferent to him and leave him to draw what conclusions he pleases.

A slight pause.

COLLIE I've got an awful headache. *(Moving down right)* I wonder if you'd tell the others that I can't play tennis again to-day. Perhaps Ethel will make a four.

EVA *(moving to right center, above chair 3)* Oh, my dear, I am sorry. Of course you mustn't play. That's quite all right.

LEONARD ARDSLEY *comes out from the house. He is a red-faced, hearty man of sixty-five, with blue eyes and white hair. He looks more like the old fashioned sporting squire than the country solicitor. He is on familiar terms with the local gentry and in the season enjoys a day's shooting.*

(turning to ARDSLEY*)* Oh, there you are, father. We've all had tea.

ARDSLEY *(moving down below chair 4)* I had somebody with me. *(With a nod to* COLLIE*)* How are you, Stratton? Run along, Evie, I'll help myself. I want to have a word with our young friend. *(He sits, and pours out his tea)*

EVA *(crossing right)* Oh, all right.

She goes out into the garden.

ARDSLEY I've just seen Radley.

COLLIE *(moving to below chair 3)* Yes.

ARDSLEY *(stirring his tea)* I'm afraid I haven't got very good news for you.

COLLIE He won't wait?

ARDSLEY He can't wait. *(He sips his tea)*

COLLIE Then what's to be done?

ARDSLEY The only sensible thing is to file your petition.

COLLIE *(moving up center)* It's ridiculous. *(Turning, right of chair 4)* It's only a matter of a hundred and eighty-seven pounds. I'm sure if I can hang on a little longer I can manage. When does Radley want to be paid?

ARDSLEY The first of the month.

COLLIE I've just got to get the money before then, that's all.

ARDSLEY *(rising)* You've had a hard struggle and you've deserved to succeed. *(Patting* COLLIE *on the shoulder)*

Believe me, no one will be sorrier than I if you're beaten. You know, you needn't worry about my fees. We'll forget about them.

COLLIE That's very kind of you.

ARDSLEY Not a bit of it. *(To below chair 4, pouring out more tea)* I think it's very tough on you fellows out of the services. A man with your record. *(Turning to COLLIE)* You put all your eggs in the one basket, didn't you?

COLLIE Everything. If I go bust I haven't a shilling. *(Moving away to right center)* I'll be thankful if I can get a job driving a motor bus.

ARDSLEY *(cheerily)* Oh, I hope it won't come to that. *(Business with cake, etc)* It would be rather a come-down for a man who's commanded a destroyer and has all the ribands you have.

MRS ARDSLEY *enters up center from the house with* DR. PRENTICE. *He is a thin, elderly man with iron-grey hair, a stern face and searching eyes.*

Hulloa, Charlie.

PRENTICE How are you? Oh, Stratton. *(He moves left, above the table)*

ARDSLEY Just in time for a cup of tea. *(To COLLIE)* Don't you bother about us if you want to go and play tennis.

COLLIE No, I'm not playing any more. I'll hop it. Good-bye, Mrs Ardsley.

MRS ARDSLEY *(up left center)* Are you going already?

COLLIE I'm afraid I must.

MRS ARDSLEY Well, good-bye. *(They shake hands)* Come again soon.

COLLIE Good-bye.

He nods to the two men and exits up center.

MRS ARDSLEY *(to* PRENTICE*)* Will you have some tea?

PRENTICE No, thank you.

A slight pause.

MRS ARDSLEY *(to chair 3)* Collie looks rather worried. *(She sits)* Is anything the matter?

PRENTICE *(crossing to center)* I'm told his garage isn't doing any too well.

ARDSLEY *(sitting in the chair 4)* It's the same old story. All these ex-officers. They go into business without knowing anything about it. And by the time they've learnt how many beans make five they've lost every bob they'd got. *(He proceeds with his tea)*

MRS ARDSLEY It's very hard on them.

ARDSLEY Of course it is. But what's to be done about it? The nation can't afford itself the luxury of supporting an army of officers it has no use for.

PRENTICE *(crossing above* MRS ARDSLEY *to seat 2)* The unfortunate thing is that the lives they've led in the service have unfitted them for the rough and tumble of ordinary life.

ARDSLEY *(putting back his cup)* Well, I must get back to my office. Is this just a friendly call, Charlie, or are you hunting a patient? Personally, I am in robust health, thank you very much.

PRENTICE *(with grim humour)* That's what you say. I expect your blood pressure's awful.

ARDSLEY Get along with you. I've never had a day's illness in my life.

PRENTICE Well, don't blame me if you have a stroke. I always have my suspicions about a man who looks as well as you do.

MRS ARDSLEY As a matter of fact, I wanted to have a little talk with you, Charlie, about Eva. She's been very jumpy lately.

ARDSLEY Oh, that's only your fancy, my dear. She's getting a little old maidish. The great thing is to give her occupation. Fortunately Sydney gives her plenty to do.

PRENTICE Sydney keeping pretty fit?

MRS ARDSLEY As fit as can be expected.

ARDSLEY *(rising)* Poor old Sydney. *(He moves to center)* The only thing we can do is to make things as easy for him as we can. It's been a great blow to me. I was hoping he'd go into the business. He'd have been able to take a lot of the work off my hands now. I've paid for the war all right.

PRENTICE *(with a twinkle in his eye)* He has, too, in a way.

ARDSLEY Of course. But he's got used to it. Invalids do, you know. Well, it's lucky I've got my health and strength. Anyhow, I must go back and do a job of work.

He nods to PRENTICE *and exits up center.*

PRENTICE *(sitting on seat 2)* Leonard's a wonderful fellow. He always looks at the bright side of things. *(During the following dialogue, he loads and lights his pipe)*

MRS ARDSLEY It's a strength.

PRENTICE You've spoilt him.

MRS ARDSLEY I've loved him.

PRENTICE I wonder why.

MRS ARDSLEY *(with a smile)* I can't imagine. I suppose because he can never see further than the end of his nose and I've always had to take care that he didn't trip over the obvious and hurt himself.

PRENTICE You've been a good wife and mother, Charlotte. There aren't many left like you now.

MRS ARDSLEY Times are difficult. I think one should make allowances for all these young things who are faced with problems that we never dreamed of.

PRENTICE What did you want to say to me about Evie?

MRS ARDSLEY I want her to come and see you. She's been losing weight. I'm rather uneasy about her.

PRENTICE I daresay she wants a holiday. I'll have a talk to her. *(He pauses, pressing down his tobacco)* But you know I'm more concerned about you. I don't like this pain you've been complaining of.

MRS ARDSLEY I don't think it's very important. *(Taking up her needlework)* It's just pain, you know. I suppose most women of my age have it now and then.

PRENTICE I've been thinking about it. I want you to let me make a proper examination.

MRS ARDSLEY I'd hate it.

PRENTICE I'm not a bad doctor, you know, even though I am your brother.

MRS ARDSLEY You can't do anything for me. When the pain gets bad I take some aspirin. It's no good making a fuss.

PRENTICE If you won't let me examine you I shall go to Leonard.

MRS ARDSLEY No, don't do that. He'll have a fit.

PRENTICE Come along, then.

MRS ARDSLEY Now?

PRENTICE Yes, now.

MRS ARDSLEY *(after a slight pause)* I disliked you when you were a little boy and used to make me bowl to you, and every year that has passed since then has made me dislike you more.

PRENTICE You're a wrinkled old hag, Charlotte, and women ought to be young and pretty, but upon my word there's something about you that I can't help liking.

MRS ARDSLEY *(smiling)* You fool.

LOIS *and* WILFRED CEDAR *saunter in right, from the garden.*

LOIS Hulloa, Uncle Charlie. *(Crossing left, to below the table)* Tennis is off. Evie says Collie's got a bad head. *(She takes a piece of cake)*

MRS ARDSLEY He's gone home.

PRENTICE *(rising)* I'm just taking your mother off to have a look at her. *(He turns up center)*

LOIS Oh, mother, you're not ill?

MRS ARDSLEY *(rising)* No, darling, of course not. *(Moving up to the house)* Uncle Charlie's an old fuss-pot.

She exits center, with PRENTICE.

WILFRED *(at right)* D'you want me to take myself off?

LOIS No, sit down. *(She sits in chair 7)* Would you like a drink?

WILFRED *(crossing to right of the table)* Not at the moment. Let's have a talk.

LOIS The days are drawing in. Oh, how I hate the winter.

WILFRED It must be pretty grim down here. *(He sits in chair 4)*

LOIS The wind! When d'you go south?

WILFRED Oh, not for another month.

LOIS Shall you take a house here again next year?

WILFRED I don't know. Would you like me to?

LOIS Naturally. It's awful when there's no one at the Manor.

WILFRED *(after a slight pause, regarding her)* D'you know, you're a very pretty girl.

LOIS It doesn't do me much good.

WILFRED I wonder you don't go on the stage.

LOIS One can't "go on the stage" just like that.

WILFRED With your looks you could always get a job in the chorus.

LOIS Can you see father's face if I suggested it?

WILFRED You haven't got much chance of marrying in a place like this.

LOIS Oh, I don't know. Someone may turn up.

WILFRED I believe you'd be a success on the stage.

LOIS One has to have training. At least a year. I'd have to live in London. It costs money.

A pause. WILFRED *rises.*

WILFRED I'll pay.

LOIS *(after looking at him in silence)* You? What *do* you mean?

WILFRED Well, I'm not exactly a poor man. I can't bear the thought of your going to seed in a rotten little hole like this.

LOIS Don't be silly. How can I take money from you?

WILFRED Why not? *(Turning up to above the table)* I mean, it's absurd at this time of day to be conventional.

LOIS What do you think Gwen would say?

WILFRED She needn't know.

LOIS Anyhow, it's too late. I'm twenty-six. One has to start at eighteen... It's extraordinary how the years slip by. I didn't realise I was grown up till I was twenty. I vaguely thought of becoming a typist or a hospital nurse. But I never got beyond thinking of it. I suppose I thought I'd marry.

WILFRED What'll you do if you don't?

LOIS Become an old maid. Be the solace of my parents' declining years.

WILFRED I don't think much of that.

LOIS I'm not complaining, you know. Life's so monotonous here. Time slips by without your noticing it.

WILFRED *(sitting against the left arm of chair 5)* Has no one ever asked you to marry him?

LOIS Oh, yes. An assistant of Uncle Charlie's did. An odious little man. And there was a widower with three children and no money. I didn't think that much catch.

WILFRED I don't blame you.

LOIS What made you suggest that just now? Paying for my training?

WILFRED Oh, I don't know. I was sorry for you.

LOIS You don't give me the impression of a philanthropist.

WILFRED *(standing)* Well, if you must know, I'm crazy about you.

LOIS And you thought I'd show my gratitude in the usual way.

WILFRED I never thought about it.

LOIS *(rising, and moving to center)* Oh, come off it.

WILFRED *(to above chair 4)* You're not angry with me?

   LOIS *turns to him.*

It's not my fault if I'm just dotty about you.

LOIS After all, you are old enough to be my father.

WILFRED I know. You needn't rub it in.

LOIS I think it's just as well that you're going away in a month.

WILFRED *(moving towards her)* I'd do anything in the world for you, Lois.

LOIS *(crossing him, to left)* Thank you very much, but there's nothing you can do.

She turns below and left of the table.

WILFRED You don't know what you're talking about. You're just mouldering away here. I can give you a better time than you've ever dreamed of. Paris. You've never been there, have you? By God, you'd go mad over the clothes. You could buy as many as you liked. Cannes and Monte. And what price Venice? Gwen and I spent the summer before last at the Lido. It was a riot, I can tell you.

LOIS You're a monstrous old man. If I were a properly brought up young woman I should ring for a flunkey and have you shown the door.

WILFRED I'm not a bad sort. I'm sure I could make you happy. You know, you could turn me round your little finger.

LOIS *(looking at her fingers)* Blazing with jewels?

WILFRED Rather.

LOIS *(with a laugh)* You fool.

WILFRED *(taking a pace or two towards the table)* God, how I love you. It's a relief to be able to say it, at all events. I can't make out how you never guessed it.

LOIS It never occurred to me. Does Gwen know?

WILFRED Oh, no, she never sees anything. She hasn't got the brains of a louse.

LOIS You're not going to make a nuisance of yourself, are you?

WILFRED No, I'm going to leave you to think about it.

LOIS That's not necessary. There's nothing doing. I can tell you that at once.

As he takes a pace towards her.

Take care, there's someone coming.

WILFRED *turns right, and moves up, above chair 4.*
HOWARD BARTLETT *enters center, from the house. He is a big, fine man of forty, somewhat on the stout side, but still with the dashing good looks that had attracted* ETHEL *during the war. He wears rather shabby plus-fours and a golf coat of rather too loud a pattern. He is altogether a little showy. He does not drop his aitches*

often, but his accent is slightly common. At the moment he is not quite sober. You would not say he was drunk, but the liquor he has had during the day has made him jovial.

HOWARD *(moving down to right of chair 4)* Well, here I am.

LOIS Hulloa, Howard.

HOWARD I've caught you, have I?

WILFRED *moves to left of chair 5.*

What are you doing with my sister-in-law, Cedar? Eh? You be careful of that man, Lois. He's up to no good.

LOIS *(with a laugh)* Oh, shut up, Howard.

HOWARD I know him. He's just the kind of fellow to lead a poor girl astray.

LOIS *(coolly)* Howard, you've had a couple.

HOWARD *(easing right, to center)* I know I have, and I'm feeling all the better for it. *(Turning and harking back)* Don't you listen to a word he says. He's a wicked old man. *(He moves down right center, to right of chair 3)*

WILFRED *(easing to left center)* Go on. I like flattery.

HOWARD *(to LOIS)* You know, his intentions aren't honourable. *(To WILFRED)* Now, as one man to another, are your intentions honourable?

WILFRED *(moving down to left of chair 3)* If you put it like that...

HOWARD One man to another, mind you.

WILFRED I don't mind telling you they're not.

HOWARD There, Lois, what did I tell you?

LOIS At all events I know where I am now.

HOWARD *(crossing WILFRED, to right of LOIS)* Don't say I didn't warn you. When you're walking the streets of London, with a baby on your arm and no home to go to, don't say, Howard never warned me.

LOIS Ethel's waiting for you, Howard. She wants to go home.

HOWARD No place like home and home's a woman's place.

LOIS You'll find her somewhere in the garden.

HOWARD A good woman. You always know where to find her. She's not one of your gad-abouts. One of the best. And a lady, mind you. *(To* **WILFRED***)* I don't mind telling you I'm not a gentleman by birth.

WILFRED Aren't you? *(He eases to below and right of chair 3)*

HOWARD The King made me a gentleman. His Majesty. I may be only a farmer now, but I've been an officer and a gentleman. And don't you forget it.

LOIS You're drivelling, Howard. *(She moves away above chair 7)*

HOWARD *(crossing back to* **WILFRED***)* What I mean to say is, leave the girl alone, Cedar. A poor motherless child. An innocent village maiden. I appeal to your better nature.

WILFRED D'you know what's the matter with you, Bartlett?

HOWARD I do not.

WILFRED You're tight.

HOWARD Me? I'm as sober as a judge. How many drinks d'you think I've had to-day?

WILFRED More than you can count.

HOWARD On the fingers of one hand, maybe. *(With triumph)* But not on the fingers of two. It wants more than that to make me tight. *(He sits in chair 3)*

WILFRED You're getting older. You can't carry your liquor like you used to.

HOWARD Do you know, when I was an officer and a gentleman, I could drink a bottle of whisky at a sitting and not turn a hair.

He turns in his chair and sees **MRS ARDSLEY** *and* **DR. PRENTICE** *coming through the drawing-room.*

Here's the Doctor. We'll ask him.

MRS ARDSLEY *and* **DR. PRENTICE** *enter center.*

MRS ARDSLEY *(moving down right center)* Oh, Howard, I didn't know you were here.

HOWARD As large as life.

PRENTICE *(moving down to the table)* Been into Stanbury?

HOWARD Market-day to-day.

PRENTICE Do any business? *(He sits in chair 5)*

HOWARD Business is rotten. Just wasting my time, I am. Farming's gone all to hell.

MRS ARDSLEY You look tired, Howard. Would you like me to have a cup of tea made for you?

HOWARD Tired? I'm never tired. *(Pointing to* **WILFRED***)* Do you know what this chap says? He says I'm tight.

MRS ARDSLEY *sits in chair left.*

WILFRED I was only joking.

HOWARD *(solemnly)* I'm going to get a professional opinion. *(Rising and moving to left center)* Uncle Charlie and Dr. Prentice, as one man to another, tell me, am I tight? Don't mind hurting my feelings. I'll bear it, whatever you say, like an officer and a gentleman. *(Pulling himself erect)* Shun!

PRENTICE I've seen men a lot tighter.

HOWARD You examine me. I want to get to the bottom of this. Tell me to say British Constitution.

PRENTICE Say British Constitution.

HOWARD I've already said it. You can't catch me that way. Now what about the chalk line?

PRENTICE What about it?

HOWARD Look here, do you want me to teach you your business? Draw a chalk line and make me walk along it. That'll prove it. Go on. Draw a chalk line. Draw it straight, mind you.

PRENTICE I don't happen to have any chalk.

HOWARD You haven't got any chalk?

PRENTICE No.

HOWARD Then I shall never know if I'm tight or not. *(He sits in chair 4)*

SYDNEY *enters right from the garden, accompanied by* ETHEL. *A moment later* EVA *follows them.*

ETHEL *(moving in, to right center)* Howard. Had a good day? *(She crosses to above and right of chair 4)*

SYDNEY Hulloa. *(He moves up and sits left of* WILFRED *on seat 2)*

HOWARD Yes, I met a lot of good chaps, white men, fine upstanding fellows. Straight as a die. Pick of the British nation.

ETHEL *gives a little start as she realises that he is tipsy but pretends to notice nothing and moves away to chair 3.*

ETHEL *(brightly)* How was business?

HOWARD Rotten. Everybody's broke. Farming—what a game! What I ask you is, why the Government don't do something?

During the following, EVA *moves across and up right. She moves chair 6 a little right, nearer chair 5.*

ETHEL Well, they've promised to.

HOWARD Are they going to keep their promises? You know they're not, I know they're not, and they know they're not.

ETHEL Then the only thing is to grin and bear it as we've grinned and borne it all these years.

HOWARD Are we the backbone of the country or not?

SYDNEY I've never heard a Member of Parliament who didn't say so.

HOWARD *(about to get angry)* I know what I'm talking about.

ETHEL *(soothingly)* Of course you do.

HOWARD *(rising)* Then why does he contradict me? *(He moves to right of chair 3)*

SYDNEY I wasn't contradicting you. I was agreeing with you.

HOWARD *(mollified)* Were you, old boy? Well, that's damned nice of you. You're a sport. I've always liked you, Sydney.

ETHEL *moves to chair 4, and sits.*

SYDNEY Good.

HOWARD *(right center)* I was born on a farm. Born and bred. Except when I was an officer and a gentleman, I've been a farmer all me life. Shall I tell you what's wrong with farming?

SYDNEY No.

HOWARD No?

SYDNEY No.

HOWARD *(turning away)* All right, I won't. *(He sinks back, comatose, into chair 3)*

At that moment **GWEN CEDAR** *comes in from the drawing-room. She has a fixed bright smile on her face.*

MRS ARDSLEY *(a little surprised)* Oh, Gwen.

GWEN I'm like a bad penny. *(She crosses down right to* **MRS ARDSLEY***)* I was just passing your door and the maid told me Wilfred was still here, so I thought I'd step in for him.

MRS ARDSLEY Of course.

WILFRED's *face is sullen with anger.*

WILFRED What's the idea, Gwen?

GWEN *(turning, below seat 2)* I didn't think you'd want to walk all that way.

WILFRED You said you were going home.

GWEN I remembered I had some things to do.

WILFRED I prefer to walk.

GWEN *(with a bright smile)* Why?

WILFRED Good God, surely I don't have to explain why I want to walk.

GWEN It seems so silly when the car is there.

WILFRED I need the exercise.

GWEN You've had lots of exercise.

WILFRED You're making a fool of yourself, Gwen.

GWEN How rude you are, Wilfred.

WILFRED It's maddening that you can never trust me out of your sight for ten minutes.

GWEN *(still very bright)* You're so fascinating. I'm always afraid some bold bad woman will be running after you.

WILFRED *(in a surly tone, rising)* Come on, then. Let's go.

GWEN *(turning to shake hands with **MRS ARDSLEY**)* Tiresome creatures men are, aren't they?

WILFRED Good-bye, Mrs Ardsley. Thank you very much. *(He moves up right center)*

GWEN It's been a lovely afternoon. So kind of you to ask us.

MRS ARDSLEY *(rising)* I hope you'll come again very soon.

They shake hands.

WILFRED *gives a sullen nod to the others. He waits at the window for his wife and when she flutters out he follows her.*

SYDNEY *(moving to below seat 2)* What's the trouble?

LOIS What a fool of a woman.

SYDNEY *(sitting)* I bet he gives her hell in the car.

PRENTICE *rises, and moves to the flower bed left of the windows.* **HOWARD** *gives a little snore. He has fallen into a drunken sleep.* **ETHEL** *gives a start.*

ETHEL Listen to Howard. He's tired out, poor dear. One of the cows has something the matter with her and he was up at five this morning.

MRS ARDSLEY *(moving up center)* Let him sleep for a little, Ethel. Sydney, hadn't you better come in? It's beginning to get quite chilly.

SYDNEY *(rising)* All right.

MRS ARDSLEY, DR. PRENTICE *and* **SYDNEY** *go off into the house.*

PRENTICE *(to* **SYDNEY**, *as they go)* How has the neuralgia been lately?

SYDNEY Bearable, you know.

MRS ARDSLEY's *three daughters are left with the drunken sleeping man.*

ETHEL *(after a pause)* Poor Howard, he works so hard. I'm glad to see him get a few minutes' rest.

EVA You work hard too and you get no rest.

ETHEL I love it. I'm so interested in it, and Howard's a wonderful person to work with.

EVA Would you marry him over again if you could put the clock back?

ETHEL Why, of course. He's been a wonderful husband.

    MRS ARDSLEY *comes to the french windows.*

MRS ARDSLEY Evie, Sydney would like a game of chess.

EVA All right, mother. I'll come.

    MRS ARDSLEY *withdraws into the room.*

LOIS Don't you hate chess?

EVA I loathe it. *(She rises and moves to above and right of chair 5)*

ETHEL Poor Evie.

EVA *(setting chairs in to the table, fidgeting with the tea things)* It's one of the few games Sydney can play. I'm glad to do anything I can to make life a little easier for him.

ETHEL That horrible war.

LOIS *(rising, and crossing slowly to center)* And the chances are that it'll go on like this till we're all weary old women.

    She regards HOWARD, *who gives another snore.*

EVA *(turning from the table)* I'll go.

    She makes her way into the house.

LOIS *(after a pause, turning to* ETHEL*)* At all events you've got your children.

ETHEL I've got nothing to complain of.

    LOIS *moves to* ETHEL, *and bending over her, kisses her on the cheek. Then she saunters away into the darkening garden.* ETHEL *looks at her husband and the tears flow down her cheeks. She takes out her handkerchief and nervously pulls it about as she tries to control herself.*

    Curtain.

ACT II

SCENE—The dining-room of the ARDSLEYs' *house, about two weeks later.*

It is furnished in an old-fashioned style, with a mahogany sideboard, mahogany chairs with leather seats and backs, and a solid mahogany dining-table. On each side of the fireplace, right, is an easy chair, one with arms for the master of the house and one without for the mistress. On the walls are large framed engravings of academy pictures. The door to the hall is up right. See the Ground Plan.

There is a bow window left, looking on the High Street, and here EVA *and* SYDNEY *are seated, at a round table, playing chess. Luncheon is just over and* GERTRUDE, *the maid, above and left of table, is clearing away.* MRS ARDSLEY *is sitting in her easy chair, down right, reading the paper.*

EVA Uncle Charlie's car has just driven up.

SYDNEY Do attend to the game, Evie.

EVA It's your move.

MRS ARDSLEY You'd better go and open the door, Gertrude.

GERTRUDE Very good, ma'am.

She exits.

EVA He's been here rather often lately.

MRS ARDSLEY You know what he is. He will fuss.

SYDNEY You're not ill, mother, are you?

MRS ARDSLEY No, only old.

SYDNEY I doubt whether even Uncle Charlie can do much about that.

MRS ARDSLEY That's what I tell him.

GERTRUDE *shows in* DR. PRENTICE.

GERTRUDE Dr. Prentice.

He comes down, kisses MRS ARDSLEY, *who has risen and moved up, and waves to the others.*

PRENTICE How are you? Don't let me disturb your game.

GERTRUDE *has gone to the sideboard, and now comes back to above the table center, clearing away.*

SYDNEY D'you want us to leave you?

PRENTICE No. This isn't a doctor's visit. I'm only stopping a minute.

MRS ARDSLEY *moves up to the small table and puts down the newspaper.*

SYDNEY Queen's knight to queen's bishop third.

EVA *moves the piece he indicates. The Doctor crosses* MRS ARDSLEY *and holds out his hands to the fire.*

PRENTICE Chilly to-day.

MRS ARDSLEY *(coming down left of* DR. PRENTICE*)* Have you arranged something?

PRENTICE Yes, three o'clock to-morrow afternoon.

MRS ARDSLEY That'll suit very well. *(She sits in chair 2)*

PRENTICE *(turning, his back to the fire)* Where's Lois?

MRS ARDSLEY She's playing golf. She thought it would be a rush to get back, so she lunched at the club house.

SYDNEY She's playing with Wilfred. She said she'd bring him
back with her and Collie's coming in so that we can have a
rubber or two of bridge.

MRS ARDSLEY Oh, that'll be nice for you, Sydney.

SYDNEY Is there a fire in the drawing-room?

MRS ARDSLEY I'll have one lit. Gertrude.

GERTRUDE *has been clearing the rest of the things on
to a tray, and now has finished.*

GERTRUDE Very good, ma'am.

*She puts the table-cloth away in the sideboard drawer,
fetches the tray from the table, and goes out.*

MRS ARDSLEY *(to* DR. PRENTICE*)* Can't you stay and have a
man's four?

PRENTICE I wish I could. I'm too busy.

EVA King's knight to queen's third.

SYDNEY That's an idiotic move, Evie.

EVA *(sharply)* There's no reason why I shouldn't make it if I
want to.

SYDNEY You must protect your bishop.

EVA Play your own game and let me play mine.

MRS ARDSLEY Evie.

SYDNEY You won't look ahead.

EVA *(violently)* Good God, don't I spend my life looking ahead?
And a damned cheerful prospect it is.

SYDNEY My dear, what on earth's the matter with you?

EVA *(regaining her self-control)* Oh, nothing. I'm sorry.
I'll protect my bishop. Queen's bishop's pawn to bishop's
fourth.

SYDNEY I'm afraid that's not a very good move.

EVA It'll do.

SYDNEY There's not the least use playing chess unless you're prepared to give it some attention.

EVA Oh, can't you stop nagging? It's enough to drive one insane.

SYDNEY I didn't mean to nag. I won't say another word.

EVA Oh, I'm sick of it.

She rises, takes the board and throws all the pieces on the floor.

MRS ARDSLEY Evie!

EVA *(crossing to chair 4, down center)* Damn it! Damn it! Damn it! *(She sits)*

MRS ARDSLEY *(rising and crossing to EVA)* Evie, what's the matter with you? You mustn't lose your temper because you're losing a game. That's childish.

EVA As if I cared whether I lost or won. I hate the filthy game.

PRENTICE *(moving down a little; soothingly)* I think it's very boring myself. *(He sits on chair left)*

MRS ARDSLEY Sydney has so few amusements.

EVA Why should I be sacrificed all the time?

SYDNEY *(with an amused smile)* My dear, we thought you liked it.

EVA I'm sick of being a drudge.

MRS ARDSLEY I'm sorry, I never knew you looked at it like that. I thought you wanted to do everything you could for Sydney.

EVA I'm very sorry he's blind. But it's not my fault. I'm not responsible for the war. He ought to go into a home.

MRS ARDSLEY Oh, how cruel. How callous.

EVA He took his chance like the rest of them. He's lucky not to have been killed.

SYDNEY That of course is a matter of opinion.

EVA It's monstrous that he should try to prevent anyone else from having a good time.

MRS ARDSLEY I thought it was a privilege to be able to do what we could to make life easier for him when he gave so much for us. And I felt that it wasn't only for him we were doing it, but also for all those others who, for our sakes, and for what at least they thought was honour, have sacrificed so much of what makes life happy and good to live.

EVA *(rising)* I've given enough. I gave the man I was going to marry. I adored him. I might have had a home of my own and children. I never had another chance. And now...now. Oh, I'm so unhappy.

Bursting into tears, she rushes out of the room. There is a moment's awkward pause.

MRS ARDSLEY *(crossing left, to pick up the chessmen)* What is the matter with her?

SYDNEY She wants a man, that's all.

MRS ARDSLEY Oh, Sydney, don't. That's horrible.

SYDNEY But not unnatural.

MRS ARDSLEY *(picking up the chessmen and putting them on the table left)* You mustn't take any notice of what she said to you.

SYDNEY *(with an indulgent smile)* Oh, my dear, I knew it already. The day's long past since I was a wounded hero for whom nothing was good enough. Fifteen years is a long time.

MRS ARDSLEY If you could bear it there's no reason why others shouldn't.

SYDNEY It was easier for me, you know. Being blind is an occupation in itself. It's astonishing how quickly the time passes. But of course it's hard on the others. At first it gives them a sort of exaltation to look after you, then it becomes a habit and they take you as a matter of course, but in the end, human nature being what it is, you become just a damned bore.

MRS ARDSLEY You'll never be a bore to me, Sydney.

SYDNEY *(affectionately)* I know. You've got that queer, incomprehensible thing that's called mother instinct.

MRS ARDSLEY I can't live for ever. It was a comfort to me to think that you'd always be safe with Evie.

SYDNEY *(almost gaily)* Oh, don't bother about me, mother, I shall be all right. They say suffering ennobles. It hasn't ennobled me. It's made me sly and cunning. Evie says I'm selfish. I am. But I'm damned artful. I know how to get people to do things for me by working on their sympathy. Evie'll settle down. I shall be as safe as a house.

MRS ARDSLEY Her not marrying and all that—it seemed so natural that she should look after you. Ethel's got her husband and children. Lois is so much younger. *(She takes the chess box and board to the window seat, left)* She doesn't understand. She's hard.

SYDNEY *(with a good-natured shrug of the shoulders)* Oh, I don't know. She's got the healthy, normal selfishness of youth. There's no harm in that. She doesn't see why she should be bothered with me, and she damned well isn't going to. I don't blame her. I know exactly where I am with her.

MRS ARDSLEY *(moving to up right, above the table)* I suppose I ought to go to Evie.

PRENTICE I'd leave her alone for a little longer.

GERTRUDE *enters with a note.*

GERTRUDE *(moving down right center)* Mrs Cedar asked me to give you this, ma'am.

MRS ARDSLEY Oh. *(She opens the letter and reads it)* Is she in the drawing-room?

GERTRUDE No, ma'am. She's waiting in her car.

MRS ARDSLEY Ask her to come in.

GERTRUDE Very good, ma'am.

> GERTRUDE *exits.*

MRS ARDSLEY How very strange.

PRENTICE What is it?

MRS ARDSLEY *(moving a little right, and down)* It's from Gwen. She asks if she can see me alone for a few minutes.

SYDNEY I'll get out then.

He rises, takes his stick, crosses above the table, and stumps towards the door.

PRENTICE *(rising)* I'll go, too. *(He crosses to above chair 3)*

MRS ARDSLEY *(at the fireplace)* I wonder what she wants.

PRENTICE Probably an address or something.

MRS ARDSLEY She could have telephoned.

> SYDNEY *exits.*

PRENTICE Am I right in thinking she's a very silly woman?

MRS ARDSLEY Quite right.

> DR. PRENTICE *has been watching* SYDNEY *go and as soon as the door is closed on him he changes his manner, and moves towards* MRS ARDSLEY.

PRENTICE I've had a long talk with Murray.

MRS ARDSLEY I hate this consultation that you've forced me into.

PRENTICE My dear, it's essential. I don't want to alarm you, but I must tell you I'm not satisfied with your condition.

MRS ARDSLEY Oh, well. It's at three o'clock to-morrow afternoon?

PRENTICE Yes. He's promised to ring me up after he's seen you.

MRS ARDSLEY *(giving him her hand)* You're very nice to me.

PRENTICE *(kissing her cheek)* I'm very fond of you.

> *He turns and goes out.* **MRS ARDSLEY** *turns thoughtfully to the fireplace. In a minute* **GERTRUDE** *shows* **GWEN CEDAR** *into the room, and after announcing her, goes out.*

GERTRUDE Mrs Cedar.

MRS ARDSLEY *(turning)* How d'you do?

GWEN *(moving down right center)* I hope you don't think it very strange my sending in a note like that. I simply had to see you.

MRS ARDSLEY Do sit down. We shan't be disturbed.

GWEN *(sitting in chair 2)* I thought I'd better talk it over with you. I mean, I thought it only fair to you.

MRS ARDSLEY Yes? *(She sits in chair left)*

GWEN I think I'd better come straight to the point.

MRS ARDSLEY *(with a little smile)* It's always a good plan.

GWEN You know that I'm Wilfred's second wife.

MRS ARDSLEY No, I didn't.

GWEN He's my second husband. We fell very much in love with one another. And there were divorce proceedings. We've been married for twelve years. It's all so long ago, I didn't see any reason to say anything about it when we came down here.

MRS ARDSLEY It was nobody's business but your own.

GWEN We've been awfully happy together. It's been a great success.

MRS ARDSLEY I imagine he's a very easy man to get on with.

GWEN Of course he's always been very attractive to women.

MRS ARDSLEY That's a thing I'm no judge about.

GWEN He's got a way with him that takes them. And he pays them all kinds of little attentions that flatter them. But of course it doesn't mean anything.

MRS ARDSLEY It seldom does.

GWEN *(rising)* All women don't know that. *(She moves away to chair 3 and turns there)* It's the kind of thing that's quite likely to turn a girl's head. It would be silly to take him seriously. After all he's a married man and *I* would never divorce him whatever he did. Never.

MRS ARDSLEY *(rising)* My dear, you said you were coming straight to the point. *(Moving up a little)* Aren't you beating about the bush a good deal?

GWEN Don't you know what I mean?

MRS ARDSLEY I haven't an idea.

GWEN I'm very relieved to hear it.

MRS ARDSLEY Won't you explain?

GWEN *(sitting in chair 3)* You won't be angry with me?

MRS ARDSLEY I shouldn't think so.

GWEN *(after a moment's hesitation)* He's been paying a lot of attention to your Lois.

MRS ARDSLEY *(with a chuckle)* Oh, my dear, don't be so ridiculous.

GWEN I know he's attracted by her.

MRS ARDSLEY How can you be so silly?

GWEN They're together all the time.

MRS ARDSLEY Nonsense. *(She sits in chair 1)* They play tennis and golf together. They're playing golf now. There are very few men for your husband to play with during the week. It's been nice for both of them. You don't mean to say you're jealous of that?

GWEN But you see, I know he's madly in love with her.

MRS ARDSLEY Oh, my dear, that's only fancy.

GWEN How do you know that she isn't in love with him?

MRS ARDSLEY He's old enough to be her father.

GWEN What does that matter?

MRS ARDSLEY A lot, I should say. I don't want to hurt your feelings, but you know, a girl of Lois's age looks upon you and me, your husband and mine, as older than God.

GWEN It isn't as if there were a lot of men here. A girl can't pick and choose in a place like this.

MRS ARDSLEY Now I'm afraid I think you're not being very polite.

GWEN I'm sorry. I don't mean to be rude. I'm so utterly miserable.

MRS ARDSLEY *(with kindness)* You poor dear. I'm sure you're mistaken. And in any case you're going away soon and that'll end it.

GWEN *(quickly)* Then you think there's something to end?

MRS ARDSLEY No, no. End your fear, I mean. I know very little about men like your husband. I daresay men of that age are often rather taken by bright young things. I think a sensible wife just shrugs her shoulders and laughs. Her safety is that the bright young things look upon her husband as an old fogey.

GWEN Oh, I hope you're right. If you only knew the agony I've been through since I found out.

MRS ARDSLEY *(rising)* I'm sure I'm right. *(She crosses to above and right of chair 3)* And if there is any truth in what you think, I'm convinced that a fortnight after you've left here he'll have forgotten all about her.

Her tone suggests an end to the conversation. GWEN *rises too. She glances towards the window, crosses to it, and sees a car stopping at the door.*

GWEN Here they are.

MRS ARDSLEY (*following to left center*) Who? (*Looking out*) Oh, your husband and Lois.

GWEN (*above the table left*) He's coming in.

MRS ARDSLEY (*below and left of the table center*) He promised Sydney to play bridge. You don't object to that, do you?

GWEN (*moving to* MRS ARDSLEY) I don't want him to see me. He'll think I'm spying on him. He'll be furious.

MRS ARDSLEY He won't come in here. He'll go into the drawing-room.

GWEN You won't say anything to Lois, will you? I don't want to put her back up.

MRS ARDSLEY Of course I won't say anything. I'm sure she's absolutely unconscious of what you've been talking about. It would only make her shy and uncomfortable.

GWEN I'll slip away the moment the coast is clear.

The door is burst open and LOIS *comes in. She is radiant with health and spirits.*

LOIS Hulloa! (*Moving down to the fireplace*) Are you here, Gwen?

GWEN Yes, your mother wanted to see me about the sale of work. I'm just going.

LOIS Wilfred is here.

GWEN (*after a slight pause*) Is he? (*Crossing above the table to up right center*) Give him my love and tell him not to be late for dinner. You're going to play bridge, aren't you?

LOIS Yes. Collie and Howard are coming. They'll have a man's four.

GWEN (*moving down a little*) Wilfred says your brother plays just as well as if he could see.

LOIS Yes, it's rather marvellous. Of course we have special cards.

GWEN *(catching sight of a pearl necklace* LOIS *has on)* Pretty chain that is you're wearing. I've never seen it before.

LOIS *(instinctively putting her hand to her neck and fingering the beads)* I bought it the other day when I went into Stanbury.

A slight pause.

GWEN How extravagant of you. I didn't know anyone could afford to buy pearls now.

LOIS It only cost a pound.

GWEN Aren't they real?

LOIS Of course not. How could they be?

GWEN *(going up to* LOIS *and feeling the pearls)* I think I know something about pearls. I would have sworn they were real.

LOIS I wish they were.

GWEN *(after regarding the pearls for a moment)* It's the most wonderful imitation I've ever seen.

LOIS They do make them marvellously now. I wonder anyone bothers to have real pearls at all.

GWEN *is taken aback. She still looks at the pearls doubtfully. Then she makes an effort over herself. She turns to* MRS ARDSLEY.

GWEN Good-bye, Mrs Ardsley. I'll have everything ready in good time.

MRS ARDSLEY *(now above and left of the table center)* Good-bye, my dear. Lois will see you out.

GWEN *and* LOIS *go out.*

MRS ARDSLEY *is left reflective. She moves above the table to right center, a little puzzled.* LOIS *comes in again, and moves down to the fireplace.*

MRS ARDSLEY *(moving to left of chair 2)* Lois dear, I've been thinking you looked rather peaked. Don't you think it would be a good idea if you went to stay at Aunt Emily's for a week or two?

LOIS I should hate it.

MRS ARDSLEY She does love having you there.

LOIS It's so incredibly boring.

MRS ARDSLEY You'll have to go before the end of the year. Much better go now and get it over.

LOIS I loathe the idea.

MRS ARDSLEY Think about it a little. I can't have you not looking your best, you know, or I shall never get you off my hands.

She turns up right, and goes out.

Her voice is heard through the still open door.

Oh, here's Collie. You'll find Sydney in the drawing-room.

As COLLIE *passes the door he sees* LOIS.

COLLIE Hulloa, Lois.

LOIS You're early.

COLLIE *(pausing in the doorway)* I had an appointment with your father, but he's had to go out. I've left a message with the clerk to say I'm here when I'm wanted.

LOIS Oh, good.

COLLIE I'll go along to the drawing-room.

LOIS Right-ho.

He passes on. LOIS *turns to the mantel mirror, and looks again at the little string round her neck. She feels the pearls.* WILFRED's *voice is heard:—"Lois!".*

LOIS Hulloa.

WILFRED *(still outside)* Where are you?

LOIS In the dining-room.

   WILFRED *appears in the doorway.*

WILFRED As Collie's here why shouldn't we start?

LOIS Howard's coming.

WILFRED I know. But there's no reason why you shouldn't play a rubber or two before he does.

LOIS Come in a minute, will you?

WILFRED Why?

LOIS Shut the door.

WILFRED *(closing the door behind him)* It's shut.

LOIS These pearls you gave me, they are false, aren't they?

WILFRED *(moving down below chair 2)* Of course.

LOIS How much did they cost?

WILFRED I told you. A pound.

LOIS Gwen's just been here.

WILFRED Why?

LOIS Oh, I don't know. She came to see mother about the sale of work.

WILFRED Oh, is that all? She's been very funny lately.

LOIS She says they're real.

WILFRED What does she know about it?

LOIS She says she knows a great deal. She has pearls of her own.

WILFRED And a pretty packet they cost me.

LOIS Is she right?

WILFRED *(pausing and smiling)* I wouldn't swear she wasn't.

LOIS Why did you say they were false?

WILFRED I didn't think you'd take them if you thought they were real.

LOIS Naturally. *(She puts her fingers to the clasp)*

WILFRED What are you going to do?

LOIS I'm going to give them back to you.

WILFRED You can't do that now. You'll give the whole show away.

LOIS There's nothing to give away.

WILFRED Oh, isn't there? You don't know Gwen. She's got the tongue of a serpent.

LOIS I can't accept a valuable pearl necklace from you.

WILFRED At all events you must go on wearing it till we go away.

LOIS How much did you pay for it?

WILFRED My dear, it's not very good manners to ask what a present costs.

LOIS Several hundred pounds?

WILFRED I shouldn't wonder.

A slight pause. Then LOIS *crosses to below chair 3.*

LOIS D'you know, I've never had a valuable thing in my life. I shall be scared stiff of losing it.

WILFRED *(moving down right a little)* Don't give it a thought. I'm not a very poor man, and if you do I shall survive it.

LOIS *(turning to him)* But I might never have known. *(Easing to right of chair 3)* I might have worn it for years under the impression it was worth nothing.

WILFRED That's what I hoped.

LOIS *(after a tiny pause; with a smile)* You know, that's rather sweet of you. I would never have thought you capable, of that.

WILFRED Why?

LOIS Well, I've always looked upon you as rather a show-off. I should have thought you the sort of man who, when he gave a present that cost a lot of money, made pretty sure that you knew it.

WILFRED That's not very flattering.

LOIS You couldn't expect me to be so awfully grateful. I mean, a string of false pearls. Howard might have bought me that when he'd won a fiver on a horse.

WILFRED I liked to think of you wearing pearls I'd given you. It gave me rather a thrill to think of them round your pretty neck.

LOIS It seems a lot to pay for it.

WILFRED *(moving towards her)* You see, I'm so terribly in love with you. Give me a kiss, Lois.

He puts his arm round her waist. He tries to kiss her lips, but she turns her face away, and he kisses her cheek.

You do like me a little, don't you?

LOIS *(coolly)* Yes. *(She eases down below chair 3)*

WILFRED D'you think you could ever love me?

LOIS It wouldn't be much use, would it?

WILFRED I'd do anything in the world for you. You know Gwen and I don't get on. We'd be much happier apart. I know I could make you happy. After all, you don't want to stay in this deadly little place all your life.

LOIS What are you asking me to do now? Run away with you?

WILFRED Why not?

LOIS *(to below the table, right of chair 4)* And be chucked the moment you were sick of me? Thank you.

WILFRED I'll settle twenty thousand pounds on you to-morrow, and if you don't like to run away with me you needn't.

LOIS *(looking at him)* Don't be such a donkey.

WILFRED Gwen would divorce me if I made it worth her while and then we'd be married.

LOIS I've always understood that when the gay seducer had worked his wicked will on the village maiden he screamed like a hyena at the thought of making an honest woman of her.

WILFRED *(moving down to her)* Oh, Lois, don't laugh at me. I love you with all my heart. Oh, I know I'm as old as the hills. I wish to God I was twenty years younger. I want you so awfully. I want you for keeps.

LOIS *looks at him for a moment seriously.*

LOIS Let's go and play bridge. *(She crosses him, and up right of the table center)*

WILFRED *eases left* **ETHEL** *enters and moves down to the fireplace.*

ETHEL Sydney's getting impatient. *(To* **WILFRED**, *humorously)* And Howard says, if you don't come along at once you'll have to marry the girl.

LOIS I didn't know you were here.

ETHEL We've only just come.

LOIS *(moving round to above the table center)* Oh, well, if Howard's here you don't want me.

WILFRED *(moving up right of the table)* All right, we'll start a rubber. *(Turning at the door)* But come and cut in later, won't you?

LOIS I must go and powder my nose.

WILFRED *exits.*

ETHEL I hear Evie's been making a scene.

LOIS Has she? What about?

ETHEL Oh, I don't know. Nerves. She ought to get married.

LOIS Whom can she marry, poor dear?

ETHEL Collie. They're just about the same age. I think it would be very suitable.

LOIS Wilfred says he's going smash.

ETHEL They could manage. Nobody's got any money nowadays, but one gets along somehow. Even a marriage that isn't quite satisfactory is better than not being married at all.

LOIS Is that your experience?

ETHEL *(facing the fire)* I wasn't talking of myself. I haven't got anything to grumble at.

A pause. LOIS *sits in chair 5.*

LOIS Wilfred wants me to run away with him.

ETHEL *(turning)* Wilfred? *(Taking a pace in, to right center)* What do you mean? Why?

LOIS He says he's in love with me.

ETHEL The dirty old man. I don't understand. What does he suggest?

LOIS Well, I suppose his idea is to keep me till he gets his divorce and then I suppose his idea is to marry me.

ETHEL The beast.

LOIS I'm getting on, you know. I'm twenty-six.

ETHEL *(aghast)* Lois.

LOIS What have I got to look forward to exactly? Getting jumpy like Eva or making the best of a bad job like you.

A pause. Then ETHEL *turns to the small table right.*

ETHEL I have my children. *(Fidgeting with the papers)* Howard has his faults like everybody else. But he's fond of me. He looks up to me. *(She sits in chair 2)*

LOIS My dear, you've got a wonderful character. I haven't. D'you think I haven't seen what a strain it is on you sometimes?

ETHEL Of course it's a hard life. I ought to have known it would be when I married a tenant farmer.

LOIS But you didn't expect he'd drink.

ETHEL I don't suppose he drinks any more than most men of his class.

LOIS Have you ever really quite got used to him?

ETHEL *(defiantly)* I don't know what you mean.

LOIS Well, he is common, isn't he?

ETHEL *(smiling)* Are you quite sure that you and I are any great shakes?

LOIS At all events we do talk the King's English. We have decent table manners and we wash.

ETHEL I don't believe you'd wash much if you had to get up at six and milk the cows. All that's convention. One oughtn't to let oneself be upset by things like that.

LOIS But aren't you?

ETHEL Sometimes. *(She pauses)* I blame myself.

LOIS What have you got in common with him, really?

ETHEL *(after a slight hesitation)* A recollection. That first year or two when I loved him so madly. He was gallant and young. He was manly. I loved him because he was of the soil and his strength had its roots in it. Nothing mattered then. Nothing that he did offended me.

LOIS My dear, you're so romantic. I'm not. Romance doesn't last. When it's dead what is left but dust and ashes?

ETHEL And the consciousness that you've done your best.

LOIS *(rising)* Oh, that. *(She crosses to left of the table)*

ETHEL It's something. I've made my bed and I'm ready to lie on it. Have you ever heard me complain?

LOIS *(looking towards the window)* Never.

ETHEL *(after a very slight pause)* I've carried my head high. I've tried to make Howard a good wife. I've tried to be a good mother to my children. Sometimes I'm inclined to be a little proud of myself.

LOIS *(turning her eyes from the window)* I suppose it's never occurred to you that it would have been better for Howard really if he'd married someone in his own class.

ETHEL Oh yes, often. That's why I feel I must always have patience with him. I ought to have known. I oughtn't to have been carried away.

LOIS My dear, you're so noble it makes me positively sick.

ETHEL *(rising)* I'm not noble at all. *(She moves down to right of chair 4)* I merely have a good deal of common sense... Lois, you're not really thinking of going away with that man?

LOIS No, not really. *(She hesitates)* It's only that it's rather exciting to have the chance.

ETHEL Oh, I'm so glad.

LEONARD ARDSLEY *comes in.*

ARDSLEY *(coming down right)* What are you two girls doing in here? Discussing frocks and frills, I'll be bound.

ETHEL *(moving to him)* How are you, father? *(She kisses him)*

ARDSLEY Chatter, chatter, chatter all day long. I know you. It's a marvel to me that you never get tired of talking about clothes. Collie's here, isn't he?

LOIS Yes, he's playing bridge.

ARDSLEY *(easing towards the fireplace)* Well, run along both of you and send him in here. I want to see him.

LOIS *(crossing above the table to center)* All right.

ARDSLEY *(to* ETHEL*)* Kiddies well?

ETHEL Oh yes. *(Moving up to the door)* They always are.

ARDSLEY Fine thing for them living on a farm like that. Grand thing, a country life.

ETHEL *(turning below the door)* They've gone back to school now.

LOIS *moves to the door, and opens it.*

ARDSLEY Of course. I remember. Best thing in the world for them. Happiest time in their lives.

ETHEL *and* LOIS *exit.*

ARDSLEY *catches sight of the ladies' paper on the easy chair and takes it up.*

I knew it.

He gives a complacent smile at his own perspicacity. The door opens and COLLIE *comes in.* ARDSLEY, *at the sight of him, assumes his professional air.*

How d'you do?

COLLIE *(moving down right center)* You weren't in when I turned up at the office just now.

ARDSLEY No. *(As he moves across to below the table center)* I've got someone waiting that I thought you'd better not meet, and I wanted to see you before I saw him. *(Turning)* So I came through my private door.

COLLIE I'm just as glad. I'm not used to solicitors' offices and I'm always rather intimidated.

ARDSLEY *(pacing back to the fireplace, and turning there)* I'm afraid I've got something very serious to say to you.

COLLIE Oh, Lord.

ARDSLEY In the three years you've been here we've seen a good deal of you. We all liked you.

COLLIE It's been a snip for me having this house to come to. Except for all of you I should have had a pretty thin time.

ARDSLEY I'm sure you'll realise that it's not very pleasant for me to find myself in my present position.

COLLIE I suppose that means the game's up. I've made a damned good fight for it. Have I got to file my petition?

ARDSLEY The bank wrote to you last month telling you that you were overdrawn and that they wouldn't cash any further cheques you drew until your account was put in order.

COLLIE Yes.

ARDSLEY And after that you gave several post-dated cheques in payment of various accounts.

COLLIE I was being pestered for money all over the shop. I couldn't help myself.

ARDSLEY You were hopelessly insolvent. How did you expect to meet them?

COLLIE I thought something would turn up.

ARDSLEY Don't you know that's a criminal offence?

COLLIE Oh, what rot. It's the sort of thing anyone might do when he was up against it.

ARDSLEY Not without going to gaol.

COLLIE Good God, you don't mean to say they're going to prosecute?

ARDSLEY You can't expect the injured parties to take it lying down?

COLLIE (*sitting in chair 3*) But it's absurd. They know I didn't mean any harm.

ARDSLEY *regards* COLLIE *for a moment.*

ARDSLEY It's almost incredible that you should be so unbusinesslike.

COLLIE What should I know about business? I'm a sailor. I was in the Navy for twenty years.

ARDSLEY I'm afraid you've been very unwise.

COLLIE *(after a slight pause)* Then what's going to happen?

ARDSLEY The bank manager is in my office now. You must be prepared for the worst, Collie. A warrant will be applied for.

A slight pause.

COLLIE Does that mean I shall be arrested?

ARDSLEY Of course you'll be released on bail. I'll arrange that. If you elect to be tried by a jury the justices will refer the case to quarter sessions. It's early days yet to decide, we'll see what counsel has to say. My own opinion at the moment is that the best thing you can do is to plead guilty and throw yourself on the mercy of the court.

COLLIE But I'm not guilty.

ARDSLEY *(with a trace of impatience)* Don't be such a fool. You're just as guilty as the thief who sneaks ten bob from your till when no one is looking.

COLLIE *(after a moment)* What will they do to me?

ARDSLEY In consideration of your previous good character and your record in the Navy, I have little doubt that the judge will be lenient. I should be very disappointed if you got more than from three to six months in the second division.

COLLIE *(with a flash of anger at the casual way he takes it)* You don't care, do you?

ARDSLEY My dear boy, don't think I'm happy about it. In my profession one often finds oneself in very disagreeable situations, but I don't remember ever having found myself in a more painful one than this.

COLLIE Fortunately most people get over seeing the other fellow come a cropper.

ARDSLEY It's not only the pleasant social relations we've had with you, but that you should have got the D.S.O. and been in command of a destroyer—it all makes your fall so much more distressing. I'm afraid it makes it also much more disgraceful.

COLLIE *(after a moment)* They'll take my D.S.O. away from me?

ARDSLEY I suppose so.

COLLIE *(rising)* I suppose it doesn't occur to you that when a fellow has served the country for twenty years in a job that's unfitted him for anything else, it's rather distressing and rather disgraceful that he should be shoved out into the world with no means of earning his living and nothing between him and starvation but a gratuity?

ARDSLEY I can't go into that. Though, of course, it's a good point to take up at the trial. I'll make a note of that. Of course the answer is that the country was up against it and had to economise and if a certain number of individuals had to suffer it can't be helped.

A slight pause.

COLLIE When I was torpedoed during the war and they fished me out, "God, what a bit of luck!" I said. I never knew. *(Moving round to below chair 4)*

ARDSLEY Do me the justice to admit that I begged you six months ago to file your petition. You wouldn't take my advice.

COLLIE *(turning to face ARDSLEY)* I'd had it drummed into me for so many years that in the Navy nothing is impossible. It was hard to give in while I still had some fight in me.

ARDSLEY You mustn't despair.

COLLIE There's not much of a future for an ex-naval officer, forty years of age, after six months in gaol.

ARDSLEY *(moving slowly towards COLLIE)* I've been a hunting man. It's a very good plan not to take your fences before you come to them. Now look here, I must be off. There's whisky and soda on the sideboard. You help yourself to a drink. I'm sure you want it.

COLLIE Thank you.

ARDSLEY *(giving him his hand)* Good-bye, my boy. I'll let you know about things as soon as I hear.

COLLIE Good-bye.

ARDSLEY *turns up right and exits.*

COLLIE, *sinking into chair 4, buries his face in his hands; but hearing the door open he looks up and pulls himself together.* EVA *comes in.* COLLIE *rises.*

EVA *(moving down)* Oh, I beg your pardon. I was looking for my bag. I didn't know anyone was here.

COLLIE I was just going.

EVA Please don't. *(She moves down towards the fireplace)* I won't disturb you. *(She turns to the small table right)*

COLLIE *(moving towards her)* What are you talking about? Surely you can come into your own dining-room.

EVA *(turning to him)* I wasn't speaking the truth. I knew you were here and my bag's upstairs. I heard father go. I wanted to see you. I'm so frightfully anxious.

COLLIE What about?

EVA Everyone knows you're in difficulties. Father let fall a hint at luncheon. I knew he was seeing you this afternoon.

COLLIE It's kind of you to bother, Evie. *(Moving away to right of chair 4)* I've had rather a rough passage, but at all events I know where I am now.

EVA Can nothing be done?

COLLIE Not very much, I'm afraid.

EVA *(coming towards him)* Won't you let me help you?

COLLIE *(with a smile, turning to her)* My dear, how can you?

EVA It's only a matter of money, isn't it?

COLLIE "Only" is good.

EVA I've got a thousand pounds that my god-mother left me. It's invested and I've always dressed myself on the interest. I could let you have that.

COLLIE I couldn't possibly take money from you. It's out of the question.

EVA Why? If I want to give it you.

COLLIE *(moving up to her)* It's awfully generous of you, but...

EVA *(interrupting)* You must know how frightfully fond I am of you.

COLLIE It's very nice of you, Evie. Besides, your father would never hear of it.

EVA It's my own money. I'm not a child.

COLLIE Can't be done, my dear.

EVA *(crossing him to right of chair 4)* Why shouldn't I buy an interest in your garage? *(Turning to him)* I mean, then it would be just an investment.

COLLIE Can you see your father's face when you suggested it? It looked all right when I bought it. Things were booming then. But the slump has killed it. It isn't worth a bob.

EVA But surely if you can get more capital you can afford to wait till times get better?

COLLIE Your father doesn't think much of me as it is. He'd think me a pretty mean skunk if he thought I'd induced you to put your money into an insolvent business.

EVA You keep on talking of father. It's nothing to do with him. It's you and I that are concerned.

COLLIE *(crossing down to her)* I know you're a damned good sort and you're always going out of your way to do things for people, but there are limits. Perhaps you'll want to get married one of these days and then you'll find your thousand pounds devilish useful.

EVA I shall never have a better use for it than to give it to someone who means so much to me as you do.

COLLIE I'm awfully sorry, God knows I want the money, but I really can't take it from anyone like you.

EVA I thought you liked me.

COLLIE I like you very much. You're a jolly good friend.

EVA I thought perhaps some day we might be more than friends.

There is a moment's silence. COLLIE *moves away.* EVA *is very nervous, but forces herself to go on. She sits on chair 4.*

After all, if we were engaged, it would be very natural that I should come to the rescue when you were in a hole.

COLLIE But we're not engaged.

EVA Why shouldn't we pretend to be? Just for a little while, I mean. Then I could lend you the money and father would help you to get straight.

COLLIE Oh, my dear, that's absurd. That's the sort of thing they do in novels. You mustn't be so romantic.

EVA You could always break it off when you got straight.

COLLIE That's not a very pretty role you're asking me to play.

EVA *(in a husky voice)* Perhaps when you got used to the idea you wouldn't want to break it off.

COLLIE My dear, what on earth ever put such an idea in your head?

EVA You're alone and I'm alone. There's no one in the world that cares twopence for either of us.

COLLIE Oh, what nonsense. Your family's devoted to you. They depend on you so enormously. Why, the whole house centres round you.

EVA *(rising)* I want to get away. *(Turning away)* I'm so unhappy here.

COLLIE I can't believe that. You're just nervous and run down. I daresay you want a bit of change.

EVA *(facing him)* You won't understand. *(Backing down a step)* How can you be so cruel?

COLLIE I'm not cruel. I'm awfully grateful to you.

EVA I can't say any more than I have. It's so humiliating.

COLLIE I'm dreadfully sorry. I don't want to hurt your feelings.

EVA After all, I'm not so old as all that. Plenty of men have wanted to marry me.

COLLIE I don't doubt that for a minute. I'm quite convinced that one of these days you'll find someone that you really like and I'm sure you'll make him a perfectly grand wife.

She moves away down left, and begins to cry. He looks at her with troubled eyes.

I'm sorry.

She sits in chair 6 and does not answer. COLLIE *turns up stage quietly and leaves the room.* EVA *sobs. Then she hears the door open and starts to her feet, turning her face away so that her tears should not be seen. The newcomer is* HOWARD. *He is quite sober.*

HOWARD *(moving down to right of chair 3)* Where's Collie?

EVA How should I know?

HOWARD We want him for bridge.

EVA *(turning on him)* Well, you can see he isn't here, can't you?

HOWARD He was here.

EVA *(stamping her foot)* Well, he isn't here now.

HOWARD Temper, temper. What price the angel of mercy now?

EVA *(moving up above and left of the table)* You're very funny, aren't you? Terribly amusing.

HOWARD I know what you've been doing. You've been asking him to marry you.

EVA *(furiously; crossing above the table to the door)* You drunken brute! Damn you! Blast you!

She flings out of the room.

HOWARD *purses his lips and grins. Then he goes over to the sideboard and helps himself to a whisky and soda. While he is sipping it* LOIS *comes in.*

LOIS Hulloa, I thought you were playing bridge. *(She moves down to left of chair 2)*

HOWARD No. Your father wanted to see Collie, and Sydney and Wilfred are having a game of piquet.

LOIS *(sitting in chair 2)* So you seized the opportunity to have a drink on the quiet. *(She takes a paper from the table and scans it)*

HOWARD My dear girl, I had to have something to pull myself together. *(He drinks)* Evie's been swearing at me. Such language, my dear. Called me a drunken brute. *(Crossing to left of* LOIS*)* I mean, it shakes a chap's morale when a properly brought-up young lady forgets herself like that.

LOIS Are you obliged to drink?

HOWARD Well, in a manner of speaking I am. My poor old father died of drink and his poor old father died of drink. So it's in the family. See?

LOIS It is rotten for Ethel.

HOWARD *(crossing down to the fire)* She has a lot to put up with, poor girl. You don't have to tell me. *(Turning, his back to the fire)* I know it. Fact is, she's too good for me.

LOIS Much.

HOWARD That's what I say. She's a lady. I mean, you only have to look at her to know that. And mind you, she never lets up. I can be a gentleman when I want to, but I don't want to all the time. I mean to say, I like to have a good old laugh now and again. She never does. Truth is, between you and me, she has no sense of humour.

LOIS I daresay after being married to you for fifteen years it's worn rather thin.

HOWARD *(after a slight pause)* I like a girl as has a bit of fun in her. Let's have a good time while we're alive, I say; we can do all the sitting quiet we want when we're dead and buried.

LOIS There's something in that.

HOWARD Mind you, I'm not complaining of Ethel. Too much of a gentleman to do that. She's class. I know that. And I'm only a common farmer. Only, you know what I mean, you don't always want to be looking up to your wife, do you?

LOIS No one asked you to marry Ethel.

HOWARD *(after regarding* LOIS *for a moment)* Pity you wasn't old enough then. I'd have married you instead.

LOIS Complimentary, aren't you?

HOWARD *(putting his glass on the mantelpiece)* You're not half the lady what Ethel is. *(Looking round at her)* And you're a bit of a devil, I shouldn't wonder. *(Moving up a little)* You and me'd get on like a house on fire.

LOIS *(rising and moving to below chair 3 with the paper)* You're drunk.

HOWARD No, I'm not. I'm cold stone sober.

LOIS *(turning)* Then I like you better drunk.

HOWARD *(moving towards her)* Give me a kiss, honey.

LOIS D'you want your face slapped?

HOWARD I don't mind.

LOIS The nerve of it.

HOWARD Come on. Be a sport.

LOIS Go to hell.

HOWARD I would with you.

> *With a sudden movement he catches hold of her and gives her a kiss full on the lips. She tears herself away from him and crosses to below and left of chair 4.*

LOIS *(as she crosses)* How dare you?

HOWARD Oh, come off it. You didn't mind. You liked it.

LOIS It almost made me sick. You stink of cows.

HOWARD A lot of girls like that. Makes them go all funny.

LOIS You filthy beast!

HOWARD Want another?

LOIS If it were't for Ethel I'd go straight to father.

HOWARD Don't make me laugh. *(He sits in chair 3)* D'you think I don't know about girls? And if you don't know about men it's high time you did. A good-looking girl like you. You ought to be ashamed of yourself. I mean, think what you're missing.

LOIS You've got a pretty good opinion of yourself, haven't you?

HOWARD And not without cause. Of course I don't say it's like the war. God, I wish it had gone on for ever. Those were the days. If you liked the look of a girl you just walked her up the garden path. Of course the uniform had a lot to do with it and being a blasted hero.

LOIS Brute. *(She turns up below chair 6)*

HOWARD *(confidentially)* Look here, why don't you come up to the farm for a few days? We could have a grand old time.

LOIS I don't know what you take me for, Howard.

HOWARD Don't talk that sort of rot to me. You're human, same as I am, aren't you? What's the good of mouldering away without having a bit of fun in your life? You come up to the farm. Now the kids have gone to boarding-school their room's empty.

LOIS *(to below the round table left)* If you're not drunk you're crazy.

HOWARD No, I'm not. You'll come, my girl.

LOIS *(looking at him, contemptuously)* And what makes you think that?

HOWARD *(rising)* I'll tell you. *(He moves towards her)* Because I want you and you know I want you and there isn't a thing that takes a girl like that. By God, I want you.

He looks at her and the violence of his desire seems heavy in the room. LOIS *instinctively puts her hand to her breast. Her breathing is oppressed. There is a silence.* MRS ARDSLEY *comes in and moves towards the small table right.*

LOIS *(recovering herself)* Oh, mother. *(She crosses* HOWARD *towards center)*

HOWARD I've just been telling this young woman she ought to come up to the farm for a few days. She looks to me as if she wanted a change.

MRS ARDSLEY *(picking up her sewing)* I'm glad you agree with me. Only a little while ago I was suggesting that she should go and stay with Aunt Emily for two or three weeks.

LOIS *(moving up right of chair 3)* I've been thinking it over, Mother. I daresay you're quite right. When d'you think I'd better go?

MRS ARDSLEY The sooner the better. To-morrow.

LOIS All right. I'll send the old girl a wire and tell her I'm coming.

MRS ARDSLEY You needn't do that. I've just written to her to say that you'll arrive in time for dinner.

LOIS Have you? You domineering old lady.

MRS ARDSLEY You're a very good girl, Lois. I didn't think you'd disregard my wishes.

LOIS I don't think I'm a very good girl. But you're a darling old mother.

She kisses her tenderly. **MRS ARDSLEY**, *smiling, pats her hand.*

Curtain.

ACT III

SCENE—*The drawing-room at the* ARDSLEYS' *house. The next day.*

It is a large low room, with french windows left leading on to the terrace that was the scene of the first act, and a door up right. See the Ground Plan.

It is furnished in an old-fashioned, commonplace and comfortable way. Nothing much has been added since it was all new when the ARDSLEYS *married. The walls are overcrowded with framed engravings and water colours, copies of Florentine bas-reliefs, weapons on wooden shields and plates in old English china. The occasional tables are laden with knick-knacks. The arm-chairs and sofas are covered with loose-covers of faded cretonne. It is a rainy, windy day and there is a fire burning on the hearth. The light is failing. It is about half-past four.*

WILFRED *is standing at the fire warming his hands.* LOIS *enters up right. She is wearing a coat and skirt.* WILFRED *turns.*

LOIS *(coming towards him with outstretched hand)* How d'you do? Mother's out. She'll be back to tea. She's gone to Stanbury.

WILFRED I know. I asked the maid if I could see you. Is it true you're going away to-day?

LOIS Yes, I'm spending a fortnight with an aunt near Canterbury.

WILFRED But in a fortnight I shall be gone.

LOIS Will you?

WILFRED Were you going without saying good-bye to me?

LOIS I thought mother would say it for me.

WILFRED *(in a husky, agitated tone)* Don't go, Lois.

LOIS *(indifferently)* Why not?

WILFRED Why are you going?

LOIS *(moving down, below the sofa)* Mother thought I wanted a change. I generally spend a fortnight with Aunt Emily once or twice a year. She's my god-mother and she says she's going to leave me something in her will.

WILFRED I was going up to London to-morrow to settle that money on you.

LOIS *(easing left)* Don't be so silly. As if I wanted that. *(Turning at left)* If I ran away with you I wouldn't take it. *(Easing right to below the sofa)* I'd rather have my independence.

WILFRED You might have given me the last fortnight. It means nothing to you. And so much to me.

LOIS *(sitting on the down-stage end of the sofa)* How did you know I was going?

WILFRED Gwen told me.

LOIS How did she know?

WILFRED Your mother rang up.

LOIS Oh!

WILFRED *(taking a step towards her)* Are you quite sure it was about the sale of work that Gwen came to see your mother yesterday?

LOIS She wouldn't have dared. You don't know mother. She'd never let anyone say a word against any of us. You've only seen her when she's being nice. She can be as stiff as a poker if one tries to take a liberty with her.

WILFRED Gwen spotted the pearls all right.

LOIS *(beginning to unclasp them)* Oh, I forgot. I can give them back to you now.

WILFRED *(sitting on her right)* Won't you keep them? Please. It can't hurt you and it'll give me so much pleasure.

LOIS I don't see how. The chances are that we shall never see one another again. As far as you're concerned it's just throwing money away.

WILFRED I want to be able to think that you're wearing something I gave you. I've held them in my hands. I want to think that they have the warmth of your body and they touch the softness of your neck.

A slight pause.

LOIS *(tempted)* I've never had anything so valuable. I suppose I'm half a strumpet.

WILFRED They only cost a pound, Lois.

LOIS Oh, you liar. Does Gwen know you gave them to me?

WILFRED She hasn't said so. She knows there's no one else who could.

LOIS Has she been making a scene?

WILFRED Oh, no, she's been holding herself in. She's afraid.

LOIS Why? Are you so terrifying?

WILFRED I don't think you'd find me so.

Another pause.

LOIS Are you awfully in love with me?

WILFRED Awfully.

LOIS Strange, isn't it? I wonder why.

WILFRED I'm broken-hearted, Lois. I know you don't love me. There's no reason why you should. But you might. If I were very kind to you. And patient. I'd do anything in the world to make you happy.

LOIS It's curious, it does give one rather a funny feeling to know someone's in love with you.

WILFRED When Gwen told me you were going, the whole world went black. She tried to say it casually, but she knew she was thrusting a dagger in my heart and she watched my face to see me writhe.

LOIS Poor Gwen. I suppose people can be rather foul when they're jealous.

WILFRED Oh, damn Gwen. I can only think of myself. You're everything in the world to me, and every one else can go to hell. It's my last chance, Lois.

She slowly shakes her head and rises, moving to right of chair 4. He looks at her for a moment with despair.

Is there nothing I can say to persuade you?

LOIS Nothing.

WILFRED I'm done. I'm finished.

LOIS I don't think so. You'll get over it. When are you going to the Riviera?

WILFRED It's only a joke to you. *(Violently)* Oh, I hate being old.

EVA *enters up right.*

EVA Why haven't the curtains been drawn? *(Seeing WILFRED)* Oh, Wilfred.

WILFRED *(rising and trying to seem naturally casual)* How are you to-day?

EVA *(by the door)* I'll turn on the lights.

She switches on the lights while LOIS draws the curtains.

LOIS It is a foul day.

EVA *moves down right.*

WILFRED I'll be getting along.

EVA Oh, aren't you going to stay to tea? Sydney's just coming. He'd love to play piquet with you.

    LOIS *moves in, to left center.*

EVA We shall be seeing you again soon, I suppose?

WILFRED *(crossing to* EVA*)* I expect so.

    They shake hands. WILFRED *turns to* LOIS, *who gives him her hand.*

LOIS Good-bye. Give my love to Gwen.

WILFRED Good-bye.

    He goes up and exits quickly.

EVA What's the matter with him? He seems all funny to-day.

LOIS I didn't notice that he was any different. *(She moves up center)*

EVA *(to the desk right)* Are you all packed up and everything? *(She fiddles with papers, etc)*

LOIS Yes.

EVA Are you taking the five-fifty?

LOIS Yes.

EVA That gives you nice time to have tea. Ethel's coming in.

LOIS I know. She wants me to take some partridges to Aunt Emily.

    SYDNEY *enters right.*

SYDNEY Tea ready? *(He moves up to chair 3)*

EVA It's not five yet. *(She sits at the desk. Business)*

SYDNEY *(sitting)* Thank God for the fire. I hate that gas stove in my room. Mother's not back yet, I suppose?

EVA No. She said she'd be in to tea.

LOIS Howard says he's expecting a very hard winter.

SYDNEY Cheerful.

LOIS Oh, I hate the winter.

EVA If it weren't for the winter we shouldn't enjoy the spring.

SYDNEY Are you obliged to say things like that, Evie?

EVA It happens to be true.

SYDNEY It happens to be true that two and two are four, but one needn't make a song and dance about it.

LOIS I'll put on the radio, shall I? *(She eases to above the table left)*

EVA Oh, for goodness' sake don't, it drives me mad.

LOIS Oh, all right.

They both give her a little look of surprise.

EVA I'm rather jumpy to-day. I suppose it's the east wind.

SYDNEY Give me my tatting, Lois, will you?

LOIS I will.

She moves to the sofa table, fetches the tatting and gives it to him. While he talks he proceeds mechanically with his work. LOIS *returns to above the sofa.*

SYDNEY I wonder if Collie will turn up?

EVA I rang up to ask him to come in to tea. He hasn't been at the garage all day.

ETHEL *and* HOWARD *enter right.*

ETHEL How's everybody? *(She moves to above chair 2)*

SYDNEY Hulloa.

HOWARD *(moving to up center)* We've brought the partridges. They'd better be hung for a couple of days. They were only shot yesterday.

SYDNEY Got many birds this year, Howard?

HOWARD A few. What's that you're doing?

SYDNEY Tatting.

EVA Put on the wireless if you want to.

HOWARD I'll put it on. *(He eases right and fiddles with the radio)*

ETHEL I'm afraid it won't be very amusing for you at Aunt Emily's.

LOIS I shall read a lot. *(She moves down to chair 4)*

Music on the radio fades in.

SYDNEY Let's hope she'll die soon and leave you a packet.

LOIS *(sitting in chair 4)* She's got very little to leave.

Suddenly **MR. ARDSLEY** *hursts into the room.*

ETHEL Oh, father.

ARDSLEY *(coming to center)* Turn off the wireless.

EVA What's the matter?

HOWARD, *who is still at the radio, switches it off.*

ARDSLEY Something dreadful's happened. I thought I'd better come in and tell you at once.

EVA *(with a cry; rising)* Collie.

ARDSLEY How d'you know?

LOIS *rises.*

SYDNEY What is it, father?

ARDSLEY They've just telephoned to me from the police station. There's been an accident. Collie's been shot.

HOWARD Shot? Whom by?

ARDSLEY I'm afraid he shot himself.

HOWARD Good God.

EVA He isn't dead?

ARDSLEY Yes.

> EVA *gives a loud, long shriek. It is a sound that is only just human.*

ETHEL Evie!

> EVA *goes up to her father with arms raised high in the air and clenched hands.*

EVA You killed him, you fiend.

ARDSLEY I? What *are* you talking about?

EVA You fiend. You beast.

ETHEL *(coming down and putting a restraining hand on her)* Evie.

EVA *(shaking her off angrily)* Leave me alone. *(To* ARDSLEY*)* You could have saved him. You devil. I hate you. I hate you.

> ETHEL *moves down right.*

ARDSLEY Are you mad, Eva?

EVA You hounded him to his death. You never gave him a chance.

ARDSLEY Good heavens, we all gave him chance after chance.

EVA It's a lie. He begged for money. He begged for time. And not one of you would help him. Not one of you remembered that he'd risked his life for you a hundred times. You brutes!

ARDSLEY Oh, what rubbish.

EVA I hope you're shamed before the whole world. Let everyone know that a brave and gallant gentleman went to his death because there wasn't a soul in this bloody place who would lend him two hundred pounds.

ARDSLEY Pretty language, Eva. In point of fact two hundred pounds wouldn't have helped him. It would have saved him from going to gaol, but that's all.

EVA *(retreating a pace)* Gaol?

ARDSLEY Yes, a warrant for his arrest was issued his morning.

EVA *(with anguish)* Poor Collie... I can't bear it! Cruel! Cruel! *(She begins to sob desperately)*

ARDSLEY Now, my dear, don't take it so much to heart. Go and lie down in your room. Ethel will come and bathe your forehead with eau-de-Cologne.

EVA crosses him to left.

Of course the whole thing is very unfortunate. No one regrets it more than I do. The poor fellow was in a hopeless mess and perhaps he took the best way out of a situation that could only have thrown discredit on the uniform he'd worn.

While he says this EVA raises her head and turns to look at him with eyes of horror.

EVA *(as she paces right, in anguish)* But he was alive and he's dead. He's gone from us for ever. He's been robbed of all the years that were before him. *(Turning at right to face ARDSLEY)* Haven't you any pity for him? He used to come here almost every day.

ARDSLEY He was a very nice fellow and a gentleman. Unfortunately he wasn't a very good business man.

EVA As if I cared if he was a good business man.

ARDSLEY There's no reason why you should. But his creditors did.

EVA He was everything in the world to me.

ARDSLEY My dear, what an exaggerated way to speak. You ought to have more sense at your age.

EVA He loved me and I loved him.

ARDSLEY *(moving away up stage)* Don't talk such nonsense.

EVA *(following him to up right center)* We were engaged to be married.

ARDSLEY *(turning, with astonishment)* What's that? Since when?

EVA Since ages.

ARDSLEY Well, my dear, you're well out of that. He was in no position to marry.

EVA *(with anguish)* It was my only chance. *(She turns away to below chair 2)*

ARDSLEY You have a good home. You'd much better stay here.

EVA And make myself useful?

ARDSLEY There's no harm in that.

EVA I've got just as much right to life and happiness as anyone else.

ARDSLEY Of course you have.

EVA You've done everything you could to prevent me from marrying.

ARDSLEY Rubbish.

EVA *(to right of the table right, and turning)* Why should I be sacrificed all the time? Why should I be at everybody's beck and call? Why should I have to do everything? I'm sick of being put upon. I'm sick of you, I'm sick of Sydney, I'm sick of Lois. I'm sick of you all.

During this speech SYDNEY *has risen.* EVA'*s agitation has become quite uncontrolled. The table by her is covered with ornaments, and now with a violent gesture she throws it over so that everything is scattered on the floor.*

ETHEL Evie!

EVA *(to right center)* Damn you! Damn you! Damn you!

Shrieking she throws herself down and hysterically beats upon the floor with her fists.

ARDSLEY Stop it. Stop it.

HOWARD *(moving down right of* EVA*)* Better get her out of here.

He picks her up and carries her out of the room. **ARDSLEY** *crosses right and opens the door. He and* **ETHEL** *follow her out.*

LOIS *and* **SYDNEY** *are left alone.* **LOIS**, *pale and trembling, has watched the scene with terror.*

LOIS What's the matter with her?

SYDNEY *(moving down right center)* Hysterics. Upset you?

LOIS I'm frightened.

SYDNEY *(turning right)* I'll telephone for Uncle Charlie. I think she wants a doctor.

He makes his way out of the room.

LOIS *stands stock-still. She cannot control the nervous trembling that seizes her.* **HOWARD** *re-enters.*

HOWARD *(moving to center)* I've put her on the dining-room sofa.

LOIS Are Ethel and father with her?

HOWARD Yes.

He looks at her and sees the condition she is in. He puts his arm round her shoulders.

Poor old girl, gave you quite a turn, didn't it?

LOIS *(unconscious of his touch)* I'm frightened.

HOWARD It's not serious, you know. Do her good to let off steam like that. You mustn't take it to heart.

A slight pause. He bends down and kisses her on the cheek.

LOIS Why do you do that?

HOWARD I don't like to see you miserable. *(She turns a little and gives him a thoughtful look. He smiles rather charmingly)* I'm quite sober.

LOIS You'd better take your arm away. Ethel can come in any minute.

HOWARD I'm terribly fond of you, Lois. Don't you like me?

LOIS *(miserably)* Not much.

HOWARD Shall I come over and see you when you're staying at Aunt Emily's?

LOIS Why should you?

HOWARD *(in a low passionate whisper)* Lois.

She looks at him for a moment, curiously and with a cold hostility. Then.

LOIS Isn't human nature funny? I know with my mind that you're a rotter. And I despise you. Isn't it lucky you can't see into my heart?

HOWARD Why, what should I see there?

LOIS Desire.

HOWARD What for? I don't know what you mean.

LOIS I didn't think you would or I shouldn't have told you. How shameful and ugly. I see that all right. It's funny, it doesn't seem to make any difference.

HOWARD Oh, I see what you mean now. That's quite O.K. Give it time, girlie. I'll wait.

LOIS *(coolly, indifferently)* You swine.

> **SYDNEY** *re-enters right.*

SYDNEY Uncle Charlie's on his way round now. *(He sits in chair 2)*

> **HOWARD** *eases up, above the sofa, and sits.*

LOIS Mother will be back in a minute.

SYDNEY How are you going to get to the station?

HOWARD I'll drive you if you like.

LOIS Oh, it's all arranged. *(She crosses towards the door)*

> **ARDSLEY** *comes in.*

ARDSLEY Prentice has come. They're putting Evie to bed.

LOIS I'll go and see if I can do anything.

> *She exits right.*

ARDSLEY *(to* **SYDNEY**, *as he crosses up to the fire)* Sydney, did you know anything about her being engaged to Collie?

SYDNEY I don't believe she was.

ARDSLEY *(turning)* D'you mean to say you think it was pure invention?

SYDNEY I shouldn't wonder. But I think she'll stick to it. After all no one can now prove she wasn't.

ARDSLEY It's a terrible thing about poor Collie. No one can be more distressed than I.

SYDNEY It seems a bit hard that after going through the war and getting a D.S.O., he should have come to this end.

ARDSLEY He may have been a very good naval officer. He was a very poor business man. That's all there is to it.

SYDNEY We might put that on his tombstone. It would make a damned good epitaph.

ARDSLEY *(moving clown a pace)* If that's a joke, Sydney, I must say I think it in very bad taste.

HOWARD *puts his feet up, and reads the paper.*

SYDNEY *(with bitter calm)* You see, I feel I have a certain right to speak. I know how dead keen we all were when the war started. Every sacrifice was worth it. We didn't say much about it because we were rather shy, but honour did mean something to us and patriotism wasn't just a word. And then, when it was all over, we did think that those of us who'd died hadn't died in vain, and those of us who were broken and shattered and knew they wouldn't be any more good in the world were buoyed up by the thought that if they'd given everything they'd given it in a great cause.

ARDSLEY And they had. *(He returns to the mantelpiece for matches)*

SYDNEY Do you still think that? I don't. I know that we were the dupes of the incompetent fools who ruled the nations. I know that we were sacrificed to their vanity, their greed and their stupidity. And the worst of it is that as far as I can tell they haven't learnt a thing. They're just as vain, they're just as greedy, they're just as stupid as they ever were. They muddle on, muddle on, and one of these days they'll muddle us all into another war. When that happens I'll tell you what I'm going to do. I'm going out into the streets and cry: "Look at me; don't be a lot of damned fools; it's all bunk what they're saying to you, about honour and patriotism and glory, bunk, bunk, bunk."

HOWARD *(putting down the paper)* Who cares if it is bunk? I had the time of my life in the war. No responsibility and plenty of money. More than I'd ever had before or ever since. All the girls you wanted and all the whisky. *(Sitting erect)* Excitement. A roughish time in the trenches, but a grand lark afterwards. I tell you it was a bitter day for me when they signed the armistice. What have I got now? Just the same old thing day after day, working my guts out to keep body and soul together. The very day war is declared I join up and the sooner the better, if you ask me. That's the life for me. By God! *(He puts his feet up again)*

ARDSLEY *(to* SYDNEY*)* You've had a lot to put up with, Sydney. I know that. But don't think you're the only one. It's been a great blow to me that you haven't been able to follow me in my business as I followed my father. Three generations, that would have been. But it wasn't to be. No one wants another war less than I do, but if it comes I'm convinced that you'll do your duty, so far as in you lies, as you did it before. It was a great grief to me that when the call came I was too old to answer. But I did what I could. I was enrolled as a special constable. *(Crossing down right to the desk)* And if I'm wanted again I shall be ready again. *(He sits)*

SYDNEY *(between his teeth)* God give me patience.

HOWARD You have a whisky and soda, old boy, and you'll feel better.

SYDNEY Will a whisky and soda make me forget poor Evie half crazy, Collie doing away with himself rather than go to gaol, and my lost sight?

ARDSLEY But, my dear boy, that's just our immediate circle. Of course we suffered, perhaps we've had more than our fair share, but we're not everyone.

SYDNEY Don't you know that all over England there are families like ours, all over Germany and all over France? We were quite content to go our peaceful way, jogging along obscurely, and happy enough. All we asked was to be left alone. Oh, it's no good talking.

ARDSLEY The fact is, Sydney, you think too much.

SYDNEY *(smiling)* I daresay you're right, father. You see, I have little else to do. I'm thinking of collecting stamps.

ARDSLEY That's a very good idea, my boy. If you go about it cleverly there's no reason why it shouldn't be a very sound investment.

MRS ARDSLEY *comes in, still wearing her hat and coat. She moves to right center* HOWARD *rises, and moves to below the sofa.*

SYDNEY Hulloa, mother.

MRS ARDSLEY *(moving to the sofa)* Hullo, dear.

As she sits down, a trifle wearily, her eye catches the litter on the floor of all the things EVA *threw over when she upset the table.*

MRS ARDSLEY Been having a picnic?

ARDSLEY Evie upset the table.

MRS ARDSLEY In play or anger?

HOWARD *(crossing to right center)* I'd better pick the things up.

MRS ARDSLEY It does look rather untidy.

He picks up one piece after the other and sets the table straight.

ARDSLEY Poor Collie's killed himself.

MRS ARDSLEY Yes, I've heard. I'm sorry.

ARDSLEY Evie's in rather a state about it.

MRS ARDSLEY Poor thing, I'll go to her.

ARDSLEY Charlie Prentice is with her.

SYDNEY Why don't you wait till you've had a cup of tea, mother? You sound tired.

MRS ARDSLEY I am rather.

DR. PRENTICE *comes in and she gives him a smile.*

Oh, Charlie. I was just coming upstairs.

PRENTICE *(to up center, by the fire)* I wouldn't. I've given Evie a hypodermic. I'd rather she were left alone.

ARDSLEY *(rising)* Take a pew, Charlie. I'm going back to my office. One or two things I want to finish up. I'll be along for tea in a quarter of an hour. *(He moves up to the door)*

MRS ARDSLEY Very well.

ARDSLEY *exits.*

HOWARD *(having finished)* There. That's all right, I think.

MRS ARDSLEY Thank you.

HOWARD *(crossing below chair 2 to the door)* I say, I think I'll just go along to Collie's garage. There are one or two bits and pieces that I've got my eye on. I'd just as soon make sure that nobody sneaks them.

SYDNEY Oh, yeah.

HOWARD *(turning at the door)* Tell Ethel I'll come back for her. I shan't be long.

He exits.

A pause.

SYDNEY What did the specialist say, mother?

MRS ARDSLEY What specialist, Sydney?

SYDNEY Come off it, darling. You don't generally favour your family with a very detailed account of your movements. When you took such pains to tell us exactly why you were going into Stanbury this afternoon, I guessed that you were going to see a specialist.

MRS ARDSLEY I never believe a word doctors say to me.

PRENTICE *(up center, his back to the fire)* Don't mind me.

MRS ARDSLEY Tell me about Evie.

PRENTICE *(to MRS ARDSLEY)* I hardly know yet. It may be it would be better if she went into a home for a few weeks.

MRS ARDSLEY She isn't mad?

PRENTICE She's very unbalanced... I was just coming round when Sydney telephoned. Murray rang me up after he'd seen you.

MRS ARDSLEY Why didn't he mind his own business?

PRENTICE It was his business.

SYDNEY Would you like me to leave you?

MRS ARDSLEY *gives him a little, thoughtful look.*

MRS ARDSLEY No, stay if you like. But go on with your tatting and pretend you don't hear.

SYDNEY All right. *(He takes his work and goes on as though absorbed in it)*

MRS ARDSLEY Don't interrupt.

PRENTICE I'm afraid Murray could only confirm my diagnosis, Charlotte.

MRS ARDSLEY *(cheerfully)* I had an idea he would, you know. You stick together, you doctors.

PRENTICE He agrees with me that an immediate operation is necessary.

MRS ARDSLEY I believe he does.

PRENTICE When I spoke to him on the telephone he said you were—hesitating a little.

MRS ARDSLEY Not at all. I didn't hesitate for a minute.

PRENTICE I'm delighted to hear it. I know your courage. I was confident in your good sense.

MRS ARDSLEY I'm glad.

PRENTICE I'll make all the arrangements and we'll have it done as soon as possible.

MRS ARDSLEY I'm not going to be operated on, Charlie.

A slight pause. **PRENTICE** *moves down center, level with* **MRS ARDSLEY.**

PRENTICE My dear, I must be frank with you. It's the only chance we have of saving your life.

MRS ARDSLEY That's not true, Charlie. It's the only chance you have of prolonging my life. For a few months or a year perhaps. And then it'll start all over again. Do you think it's worth it? I don't.

PRENTICE You have your husband and your children to think of.

MRS ARDSLEY I know. It would be a frightful expense. If I got over the operation I should always be an invalid. I should have to have a nurse. I should be much more bother than I was worth.

PRENTICE That's unkind, Charlotte. And it's untrue.

MRS ARDSLEY You've known me a great many years, Charlie. Haven't you noticed that when once I make up my mind I don't change it?

PRENTICE Don't be a damned fool, Charlotte.

MRS ARDSLEY I have nothing to complain of, I haven't had an unhappy life. I'm prepared to call it a day.

PRENTICE I don't know if Murray made himself quite clear.

MRS ARDSLEY I asked him to.

    PRENTICE *moves to the sofa, and sits below* **MRS ARDSLEY.**

PRENTICE Listen to me. I mean every word I say. If you won't consent to an operation I'm afraid you have only a few months to live.

MRS ARDSLEY *(coolly)* How odd! Those were his very words.

PRENTICE Well?

MRS ARDSLEY I've often wondered in the past how I should take it when I was told that I was going to die. I've wondered if I'd scream or faint. You know, I didn't do either. It gave me a funny sort of thrill. I felt as if I'd drunk a glass of port on an empty stomach. I had some shopping to do at Stanbury afterwards. I'm afraid I was rather extravagant. I felt so gay and light-hearted.

PRENTICE That's more than I do.

MRS ARDSLEY It shows how right Leonard is when he says it's silly to take your jumps before you come to them.

PRENTICE Oh, damn Leonard.

MRS ARDSLEY I'm free. Nothing matters very much any more. It's a very comfortable feeling.

PRENTICE And the rest?

MRS ARDSLEY Oh, the rest, my dear, is between me and the pale, distant shadow that is all you clever people have left me of God.

PRENTICE *reflects for a moment, then rises and moves down left.*

PRENTICE If you take that view of it, if you know the facts and are prepared to take the consequences, I have no more to say. Perhaps you're right. *(Turning up behind the lower end of the sofa)* I admire your courage. I should like to think that I should have enough to follow your example.

MRS ARDSLEY There is one thing I'm going to ask you to do for me.

PRENTICE My dear, anything in the world.

MRS ARDSLEY I don't want to suffer more than I need. We've always had a great deal of affection for one another, Charlie.

PRENTICE I suppose we have.

MRS ARDSLEY You doctors are a brutal lot and there's no end to the amount of pain you can bear in other people.

PRENTICE I will do everything medical practice permits me to save you from suffering.

MRS ARDSLEY *(turning on the sofa to look at him)* But I'm going to ask you to do something more.

A long, intent look passes between them.

PRENTICE I'll do even that.

MRS ARDSLEY *(with a change of manner, cheerfully)* Then that's all right. And now let's forget that I have anything the matter with me.

SYDNEY *rises and coming over to his mother bends down and kisses her on the forehead.*

As you're up you might ring the bell, Sydney. I'm simply dying for a cup of tea.

As he turns up to the fireplace and rings, **ETHEL** *comes in.*

ETHEL *(crossing to* **MRS ARDSLEY***)* I didn't know you were back, mother.

MRS ARDSLEY Yes, I got in a few minutes ago.

ETHEL *kisses her.* **SYDNEY** *eases to chair 2 and sits.*

I was going up to see Evie, but Uncle Charlie thought I'd better wait.

ETHEL She's quite comfortable.

MRS ARDSLEY Asleep?

ETHEL No, but resting.

MRS ARDSLEY Where's Lois?

ETHEL *(moving down right)* She's in her room. *(Turning chair 1 and sitting)* She's just coming.

GERTRUDE *enters with a tray.* ETHEL *carries the table above the desk below the settee and* GERTRUDE *puts the tray on it.*

MRS ARDSLEY *(to her)* Oh, Gertrude, if anyone calls I'm not at home.

GERTRUDE Very good, ma'am.

MRS ARDSLEY I don't feel inclined to cope with visitors this afternoon.

GERTRUDE *goes out.*

PRENTICE *(moving down as if to go)* I'll take myself off.

MRS ARDSLEY Don't be so stupid. You're going to stay and have a cup of tea.

PRENTICE *(checking at center)* I have other patients, you know.

MRS ARDSLEY They can wait.

LOIS *enters.* PRENTICE *returns to up center.*

You ought to be starting soon, Lois, oughtn't you?

LOIS *(moving down towards chair 4)* I've got time yet. It won't take me five minutes to get to the station.

ETHEL You won't forget the partridges?

LOIS No. *(She sits in chair 4)*

MRS ARDSLEY Give Aunt Emily my love.

PRENTICE *(easing to above the upper end of the settee)* You might remember me to her, Lois.

LOIS I will.

MRS ARDSLEY Her chrysanthemums ought to be coming on just now.

GETRUDE *re-enters.*

GERTRUDE *(above the doorway)* Mrs Cedar has called, ma'am.

MRS ARDSLEY I told you to say I wasn't at home.

GERTRUDE I said you wasn't ma'am, but she says it's very important.

MRS ARDSLEY Tiresome woman. Tell her I've just come back from Stanbury and I'm very tired. Say, will she forgive me, but I don't feel up to seeing anybody to-day.

GERTRUDE Very good, ma'am.

She is about to go when the door is burst open and GWEN *comes in. She is wrought up.* GERTRUDE *exits.*

GWEN I'm sorry to force myself on you. It's a matter of life and death. I must see you.

MRS ARDSLEY I'm not very well, Gwen. Don't you think you can wait till to-morrow?

GWEN *(moving to center)* No, no, no, to-morrow it'll be too late. Oh, God, what shall I do?

MRS ARDSLEY Well, since you're here, perhaps the best thing would be to sit down and have a cup of tea.

GWEN *(in a strangled voice)* Lois and Wilfred are going to elope.

LOIS *sits erect.*

MRS ARDSLEY Oh, my dear, don't be so silly. You're making a perfect nuisance of yourself.

GWEN It's true, I tell you, it's true.

MRS ARDSLEY Lois is going to spend a fortnight with my sister-in-law. I didn't think there was anything in what you said to me, but I didn't want any unpleasantness, so I arranged that she should be away till after you'd gone.

GWEN She's not going to your sister-in-law's. Wilfred's meeting her at Stanbury. They're going to London.

LOIS *(rising)* What are you talking about, Gwen?

GWEN I heard every word you said on the 'phone.

LOIS *(trying to hide that she is startled)* When?

GWEN Just now. Ten minutes ago. You didn't know I'd had an extension put up into my room. I'm not such a perfect fool as you thought me. Can you deny that you spoke to Wilfred?

LOIS No.

GWEN You said, "Wilfred, it's a go." And he said, "What d'you mean?" And you said, "I'm trusting myself to your tender mercies. You're for it, my boy. I'm going to elope with you."

ETHEL She was joking with him.

GWEN *(turning to* ETHEL*)* A funny joke. *(Turning again to* MRS ARDSLEY*)* He said, "My God, you don't mean it?" And she said, "I'll get out of the train at Stanbury. Meet me in the car and we'll talk it over on the way to London."

LOIS *moves up, right. Of chair 4, to above the table left.*

MRS ARDSLEY *(rising)* Is it true, Lois?

LOIS Yes.

SYDNEY You damned fool, Lois.

GWEN *(moving down center)* Oh, Lois, I've never done you any harm. I've been a good friend to you—you can't take my husband from me.

LOIS I'm not taking him from you. You lost him years ago.

GWEN You're young, you'll have plenty of chances before you're through. I'm old and he's all I've got. If he leaves me I swear to you that I'll kill myself.

MRS ARDSLEY But why have you come here? Why didn't you go to your husband?

GWEN He won't listen to me. Oh, what a fool I've been. I ought to have known when I saw the pearls.

MRS ARDSLEY What pearls?

GWEN She's wearing them now. She pretends they're false, but they're real, and he gave them to her.

MRS ARDSLEY Take them off, Lois, and give them to Gwen.

Without a word LOIS *undoes the clasp and throws the string on the table.*

GWEN Do you think I'd touch them? He hates me. Oh, it's so awful to love someone with all your heart and to know that the very sight of you maddens him beyond endurance. I went down on my knees to him. I begged him not to leave me. He said he was sick to death of me. He pushed me over. I heard the door slam. He's gone. He's gone to join her.

She falls to her knees and bursts into a passion of tears. PRENTICE *moves down towards her.*

MRS ARDSLEY Gwen, Gwen, don't give way like that.

GWEN, *still on her knees, drags herself up to* MRS ARDSLEY.

GWEN Don't let her go to him. You know what it feels like to be old. You know how defenceless one is. She'll regret it. You don't know what he's like. He'll throw her aside when he's tired of her as he's thrown all the others aside. He's hard and cruel and selfish. He's made me so miserable.

MRS ARDSLEY If that's true, if he's all you say I should have thought you were well rid of him.

GWEN I'm too old to start afresh. I'm too old to be left alone. Alone. *(She struggles up to her feet)* He's mine. I went through the divorce court to get him. I won't let him go. *(Moving to* LOIS*)* I swear to you before God that you shall never marry him. He forced his first wife to divorce him because she hadn't money, but I've got money of my own. I'll never divorce him.

LOIS Nothing would induce me to marry him.

GWEN Take him if you want to. He'll come back to me. He's old. He tries to keep up. It's all sham. I know the effort it is. He's tired to death and he won't give in. What good can he be to you? How can you be so stupid? You ought to be ashamed.

MRS ARDSLEY Gwen! Gwen!

GWEN *(down left center, turning)* Money. Oh, curse the money. He's a rich man and you haven't got a bob between you. You're all in it. All of you. You all want to get something out of it. You brutes! You, beasts!

PRENTICE *(moving down to her)* Come, Mrs Cedar, we've had enough of this. You go too far. *(He takes her arm)* You must get out of this.

GWEN *(breaking away)* I won't go. *(She crosses him to right center)*

PRENTICE If you don't, I shall put you out. *(He urges her towards the door)*

GWEN I'll make such a scandal that you'll never be able to hold up your heads again.

PRENTICE *(moving to her)* That's enough now. Get out.

GWEN Leave me alone, damn you.

PRENTICE *(taking her arm)* I'm going to take you home. Come on.

They both go out.

MRS ARDSLEY *sits on the sofa. There is a moment's awkward silence when the door is closed on them.*

LOIS *(moving to up center)* I'm sorry to have exposed you to this disgusting scene, mother.

SYDNEY You may well be.

ETHEL *(rising)* You're not really going off with that man, Lois?

LOIS *(turning at the fireplace)* I am.

ETHEL You can't be in love with him.

LOIS Of course not. If I were, d'you think I'd be such a fool as to go?

ETHEL *(aghast)* Lois!

LOIS If I loved him I'd be afraid.

ETHEL You don't know what you're doing. It would be awful and unnatural if you loved him, but there would be an excuse for you.

LOIS Has love done very much for you. Ethel?

ETHEL Me? I don't know what you mean. I married Howard. I took him for better, for worse.

LOIS You've been a good wife and a good mother. A virtuous woman. And a lot of good it's done you. I've seen you grow old and tired and hopeless. I'm frightened, Ethel, frightened.

ETHEL I wasn't obliged to marry. Mother and father were against it.

LOIS You could have stayed on at home like Evie. So can I. I'm frightened, Ethel. *(Easing to right end of the fireplace)* I'm frightened. I don't want to become like Evie.

ETHEL *(crossing to* MRS ARDSLEY*)* Mother, can't you do something? *(By the upper end of the sofa)* It's so awful. It's such madness.

MRS ARDSLEY I'm listening to what Lois has to say.

A slight pause. ETHEL *turns to* LOIS.

ETHEL *(with a catch in her breath)* You're not running away from anybody here?

LOIS *(smiling)* Oh, my dear, that isn't at all in my character.

ETHEL *(ashamed and awkward)* I thought that perhaps someone had been trying to make love to you.

LOIS *(moving a pace towards* ETHEL*)* Oh, Ethel, don't be so silly. Who is there to make love to me in this God-forsaken place?

ETHEL I didn't know. Perhaps it was only my fancy. It's just the money?

LOIS Yes, and what money brings. Freedom and opportunity.

ETHEL Those are mere words.

LOIS I'm sick of waiting for something to turn up. Time is flying and soon it'll be too late.

MRS ARDSLEY *(after a slight pause)* When did you decide, Lois?

LOIS Half an hour ago.

MRS ARDSLEY Have you considered all the consequences?

LOIS Oh, mother dear, if I did that I should stay here twiddling my thumbs till my dying day.

MRS ARDSLEY It's not a very nice thing that you're doing.

LOIS I know.

MRS ARDSLEY It's cruel to Gwen.

LOIS *(with a shrug)* I or another.

MRS ARDSLEY It'll be a dreadful blow to your father.

LOIS I'm sorry.

MRS ARDSLEY And the scandal won't be very nice for us.

LOIS I can't help it.

ETHEL It would be bad enough if you were going to be married. Gwen says she won't divorce.

LOIS I don't want to marry him.

ETHEL What's to happen to you if he chucks you?

LOIS Darling, you're years older than I am and a married woman. How can you be so innocent? Has it never occurred to you what power it gives a woman when a man is madly in love with her and she doesn't care a row of pins for him?

GERTRUDE *comes in with the teapot and the hot water on a tray, which she carries to the table by* **MRS ARDSLEY**.

MRS ARDSLEY *(to* **ETHEL***)* Go and tell your father tea is ready, Ethel.

With a disheartened gesture **ETHEL** *turns away right and goes out.*

LOIS I'll go and put on my hat.

GERTRUDE *crosses right and exits.*

(kneeling by **MRS ARDSLEY***)* I'm sorry to disappoint you, mother. I don't want to cause you pain.

MRS ARDSLEY Have you quite made up your mind, Lois?

LOIS Quite.

MRS ARDSLEY That is what I thought. Then perhaps you *had* better go and put on your hat.

LOIS *(rising)* What about father? I don't want him to make a scene.

MRS ARDSLEY I'll tell him after you've gone.

LOIS Thank you.

She goes out.

MRS ARDSLEY *and* **SYDNEY** *are left alone.*

SYDNEY Are you going to let her go, mother?

MRS ARDSLEY *(pouring milk into the cups)* How can I stop her?

SYDNEY You can tell her what the surgeon told you this afternoon.

MRS ARDSLEY Oh, my dear, with one foot in the grave it's rather late to start blackmail.

SYDNEY She wouldn't go, you know.

MRS ARDSLEY I don't think she would. I can't do that, Sydney. I shouldn't like to think of her waiting for my death. I should feel like apologising for every day I lingered on.

SYDNEY She might change her mind.

MRS ARDSLEY She's young, she has her life before her, she must do what she thinks best with it. I don't belong to life any longer. I don't think I have the right to influence her.

SYDNEY Aren't you afraid she'll come an awful cropper?

MRS ARDSLEY She's hard and selfish. I don't think she's stupid. She can take care of herself.

SYDNEY She might be a stranger, to hear you speak.

MRS ARDSLEY Does it sound unkind? You see, I feel as if nothing mattered very much any more. I've had my day. I've done what I could. Now those who come after me must shift for themselves.

SYDNEY You're not frightened at all?

MRS ARDSLEY Not a bit. I'm strangely happy. I'm rather relieved to think it's over. I'm not at home in this world of to-day. I'm pre-war. Everything's so changed now. I don't understand the new ways. To me life is like a party that was very nice to start with, but has become rather rowdy as time went one, and I'm not at all sorry to go home.

ETHEL *re-enters.*

ETHEL *(crossing to* MRS ARDSLEY*)* I've told father. He's just coming. *(She takes two cups to the table right, for* SYDNEY *and herself)*

GERTRUDE *enters with the cake stand, takes it left, and then exits.*

MRS ARDSLEY I'm afraid we've let the tea stand rather a long time.

SYDNEY Father likes nothing better than a good strong cup.

LOIS *enters. She has her hat on.*

LOIS *(startled and anxious)* Mother, Evie is coming down the stairs. *(She moves across to* **MRS ARDSLEY***)*

MRS ARDSLEY Isn't she asleep?

SYDNEY Uncle Charlie said he'd given her something.

The door is opened and **EVA** *comes in. Her eyes are bright from the drug the doctor has given her. She has a queer, fixed smile on her face. She has changed into her best frock.*

MRS ARDSLEY I thought you were lying down, Evie. They told me you didn't feel quite up to the mark.

EVA *(moving in a little)* I had to come down to tea. *(She checks right of chair 2)* Collie's coming.

LOIS *(shocked)* Collie!

EVA He'd have been so disappointed if I hadn't come.

MRS ARDSLEY You've put on your best dress.

EVA *(moving to center)* It is rather an occasion, isn't it? You see, I'm engaged to be married.

ETHEL Evie, what do you mean?

EVA *(turning to* **ETHEL***)* I'm telling you beforehand so that you should be prepared. *(Moving down to right of the table left)* Collie's coming here this afternoon to talk to father about it. *(Turning, at the table)* Don't say anything about it till he comes.

There is a moment's awkward pause. None of them knows what to say or do.

MRS ARDSLEY Let me give you your tea, darling.

EVA I don't want any tea. I'm too excited. *(She turns and catches sight of the string of pearls on the table)* What are these pearls doing here? *(She picks them up)*

LOIS You can have them if you like.

MRS ARDSLEY Lois!

LOIS *(easing to the right end of the mantelpiece)* They're mine.

EVA *(crossing slowly up to* LOIS, *with the pearls)* Can I really? It'll be an engagement present. Oh, Lois, that is sweet of you. *(She kisses* LOIS, *then turns to the mantel mirror and puts on the necklace)* Collie always says I have such a pretty neck... *(She turns away and moves down right, to below chair 1)*

MR. ARDSLEY *and* HOWARD *enter up right.*

ARDSLEY Now, what about this cup of tea? *(He crosses to center, at the fireplace)*

HOWARD *(right of chair 2)* Hulloa, Evie. All right again?

EVA Oh, yes. There's nothing the matter with me. *(She sits)*

ARDSLEY *(taking a cup from* LOIS*)* All ready to start, Lois?

LOIS *(who has eased to above the table up right)* Yes.

ARDSLEY Don't cut it too fine.

HOWARD *(moving to the tea table)* I may look you up one of these days, Lois. I've got to go over to Canterbury to see a man on business. *(Taking his cup to below and left of the sofa)* I don't suppose I shall be able to get back for the night, Ethel.

ETHEL No?

HOWARD *(turning, left of the sofa)* I'll come over and fetch you in the car, Lois, and we'll do a picture together.

LOIS *(mocking him)* That would be grand. *(She eases to right of the table up right)*

ARDSLEY *(up center, with his back to the fire)* Well, I must say it's very nice to have a cup of tea by one's own fireside and surrounded by one's family. If you come to think of it we none of us have anything very much to worry about. Of course we none of us have more money than we know what to do with, but we have our health and we have our happiness. I don't think we've got very much to complain of. Things haven't been going too well lately, but I think the world is turning the corner and we can all look forward to better times in future. This old England of ours isn't done yet and I for one believe in it and all it stands for.

EVA *rises and begins to sing in a thin cracked voice.*

EVA

GOD SAVE OUR GRACIOUS KING!
LONG LIVE OUR NOBLE KING!
GOD SAVE OUR KING!

The others look at her, petrified, in horror-struck surprise. When she stops, LOIS *gives a little cry and hurries from the room.*

Quick curtain.

FURNITURE AND PROPERTY PLOTS

ACT I

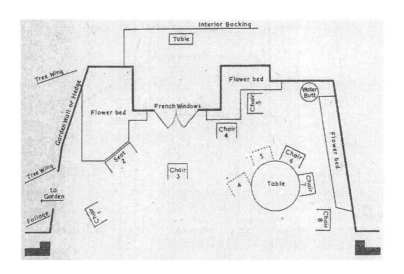

Stage cloth (to represent terrace paving).
Curtains inside french windows.
Three steamer chairs.   *(Numbered and*
Three wooden "park" chairs.   } *placed as in*
One wooden collapsible garden seat.   *ground plan and*
                                 book.)
One round table *(left).*

On it:— Tablecloth.
          Eight each of :—Cups, saucers, teaspoons, plates
          Three small knives.
          Sugar bowl *(with lump sugar).*
          Milk jug.
          Plate of cakes.
          Plate of sandwiches.

Four flower beds.
Water butt, and drain pipe.
Small table *(in backing above windows).*

On it:—Magazines, books, ashtray.

On garden seat 2:—Knitting for Mrs Ardsley.

Ready off stage, center :—
>Tea pot and hot water jug on tray (Gertrude*).*
>Two tankards of beer, on tray (Gertrude*).*

Personal :—
>Leonard Ardsley. Pipe and pouch, matches.
>Sydney. Stick.
>Ethel. Handkerchief.

ACT II

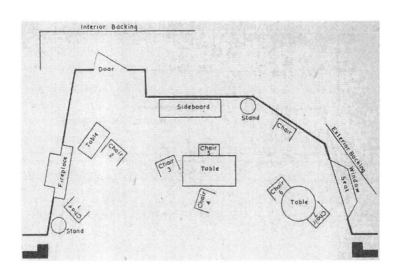

Carpet on stage. Rug at fireplace. Strip in hall backing.
Long dark curtains at the windows.

On the walls:—A few pictures; framed engravings of Academy
>pictures.

On the mantelpiece:—Knitting.
>Dining table *(center).*

On it:— Tablecloth. Cruet. Bowl of flowers.
>Round table *(left).*

On it:—	Chess board.
	Woman's magazine *(under chess board).*
	Chessmen.
	Chessmen box.
	Small table *(right, above fire).*
On it:	—Newspaper.
	Sideboard *(up center).*
On it:—	Small tray. Knives and forks. Plates. Whisky bottle. Syphon. Two glasses.
	Two stands *(down right and up left).*
On them:—	Tall vases.
	Window seat, with two cushions *(left).*
	One armchair *(above fire).*
	One small easy chair *(below the fire).*
	One small easy chair *(No. 7, down left).*
	Four dining chairs *(Nos. 3, 4, 5, 6 on plan).*
	One additional dining chair *(up left).*

Off stage, right:—
        Tray with note in envelope (Gertrude).

Personal :—'
        Lois. Pearl necklace.

ACT III

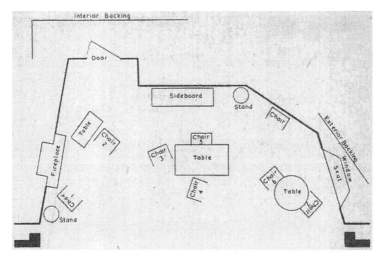

Carpet on stage. Rug at fireplace. Strip in hall backing. Long curtains at french windows *(as used in backing, Act I)*.

On the walls:—Several framed engravings. Water colours. Copies of Florentine bas-reliefs, plates in old English china. *(If available)* Weapons on wooden shields, or similar items.
One desk *(right)*.

On it:— Inkstand, writing materials, etc.
Papers and documents.
One occasional table *(above desk)*.

On it:— Several knick-knacks.
One round table *(up right center)*.

On it:— Various ornaments *(to be knocked over)*.
One sofa *(up left center)*.
One small table *(behind sofa)*.

On it:— Tatting. Newspaper. Ashtray.
One stand, or small table *(up left)*.

On it:— Radio.
One round table *(down left)*.

On it:— Three magazines. Cigarette box *(filled)*. Box of matches. Ashtray.

On the mantelpiece:—Clock. Ornaments. Box of matches. Ashtray.

Ready Offstage right :—
Table cloth
Tray with tea things for six persons $\Big\}$ (Gertrude).
Cake stand with cakes and sandwiches

Effects :—
Record of "Destiny" *(for* "radio"*)*.

LIGHTING PLOT

ACT I

Floats. Amber (or gold*)* and blue, half.
Battens. Amber (or gold*)* full, pink and blue, half.

(Towards the end of the Act the general lighting may be checked down a little, slowly, and a No. 4 amber flood faded in from O.P.)

Amber length, well checked clown, on interior backing. The room beyond the windows must be in considerable shadow.

ACT II

Floats. Amber (or gold) half, pink and blue, quarter.
Battens. Amber (or gold) three-quarters, pink and blue, half.
Exterior backing. Straw flood.
Interior backing. Lengths, amber and white.
Fire spot ON.

No Cues.

ACT III

To open:—

> *Floats.* Amber (or gold) and blue, quarter.
> *No. 1 Batten.* Amber (or gold) and blue, half. *(Other battens ditto at quarter.)*

Flood on exterior. Steel (frost*)*, checked down.
Interior backing. Amber lengths.
Fire spot ON.

At Cue:—

> *As* Eva *switches on lights:—*Bring in spots from No. 1 Batten, No. 51 gold pools on acting areas, up center, and at O.P. on and around the desk. *(If required, bring up gold in No. 1 batten by a quarter.)*